Water of an Undetermined Depth

Water of an Undetermined Depth

Richard Chiappone

STACKPOLE
BOOKS

Published by
STACKPOLE BOOKS
5067 Ritter Road
Mechanicsburg, PA 17055
www.stackpolebooks.com

Printed in the United States of America

First Edition

10 9 8 7 6 5 4 3 2 1

Library of Congress Cataloging-in-Publication Data
Water of an undetermined depth / Richard Chiappone.—1st ed.
    p. cm.
ISBN 0-8117-0033-X (hardcover)
1. Blue collar workers—Fiction. 2. Working class—Fiction.
3. Men—Fiction. I. Title.
PS3603.H52 W38 2002
813'.6—dc21

                                                                    2002008078

For Lin

Contents

Acknowledgments

———

Some of the stories in this collection appeared in the following publications:

Gray's Sporting Journal: "The Chubs," "Winter Fish," "Q Roo," "Raccoon," "Sick Baby"
Missouri Review: "Old Friend"
New Virginia Review: "Things Come to Mind"
Playboy: "Dealer's Choice"
Sou'wester: "Those Little Foreign Beauties," "Love A, Love B"
ZYZZYVA: "Maximum Reception"

"The Chubs" also appeared in the anthology *City Fishing,* and "Maximum Reception" appeared in the anthology *North of Eden.*

I would also like to thank Ron Spatz (always the mentor and always a friend) and all the others who have tried to keep me honest: Sarah Birdsall, Matt Callahan, Bob Clark, Joann Congdon, Tara Wreyford, and the rest of the old gang; the editors Jim Babb, Howard Junker, Fred W. Robbins, Evelyn Somers, and Alice Turner; and a special thanks to Judith Schnell, whose idea this book was.

What did I know, what did I know
of love's austere and lonely offices?

—Robert Hayden, "Those Winter Sundays"

The Chubs

They are ugly little fish, the chubs—four or five inches long, thick-bodied and snub-nosed, with dull eyes and rude white mouths. They are trash fish, junk fish, and their presence in a stream is a sign that something good has come to an end. But they were the only things in the sluggish little creeks around my town that would rise to my home-tied flies and clumsy self-taught casts, and for a time one spring I was a chub fisherman.

Mornings I drove my father to his job at Hooker Chemical, my textbooks on the seat between us, my rod in the trunk behind the spare tire. My father sat with his lunch pail on his lap, his hard hat between his feet. He ran his fingers up and down the spines of my books as he talked about the jobs for college students at the plant.

"Shipping," he said. "Try for shipping, or labeling. Those are the cleanest, the safest. They don't pay like production, but you're only going to be there summers. I mean, if you were coming into the plant for the long haul, God forbid, then you'd have to think seriously about the money. Capiche?"

"Labeling," I said. I was not really listening. We were in slow traffic on Buffalo Avenue. The morning sun slanted in between the factory walls, each beam of light flooded with graphite particles fluttering like a hatch of black insects. We had the windows down, and I could have closed my eyes and named the plants we passed: Carbide, reeking of rotten eggs—the sulfur dioxide that even a failure at chemistry could identify; International Graphite, smoking like a new tar roof; DuPont, its eye-watering solvents stinging the warm morning air.

We pulled up in front of Hooker, the always-leaking chlorine gas deceptively clean and bleachy smelling. The stack whistle went off with a window-rattling blast, and a flock of gray and black pigeons burst from their roosts in the pipe racks overhead. I watched them flap away around the smokestacks in a panicked curve, as if they'd never heard that whistle before, as if they hadn't spent every day of their pigeon lives right there on those shit-splattered nests.

My father glanced at his watch. "I wish I could get you into R and D. But the lab boys' kids get those jobs every time."

I said, "That's all right, Pop."

Something on the windshield had my eye. A small brown caddisfly was crawling along the wiper blade, its speckled wings folded tentlike over its back. A #12, I thought. Maybe a #14. I had both sizes in my fly box in the trunk.

"No, I mean it," my father said. "I wish I had more juice with personnel." He had the door open and was backing out. He snugged his hard hat down onto his head.

I looked at the caddis again on the windshield. Definitely a size 14. "I'm not set on anything," I shrugged.

My father shook his head. "Good Christ. You don't even know what to be afraid of."

I said, "I'm afraid I'm going to hear the story of how Bobby Dimiglio caught twelve thousand volts from the bus bars on the chlorine cell. The burns? The plastic nose they had to make for him? How he still hears buzzing every time he walks under a power line. I'm scared shitless I'm going to have to listen to that again."

He had to laugh. "College man. Smart." He picked up his lunch pail and turned to go, giving my books a little rap with his knuckles. "Anyhow," he said, "it was *thirteen* thousand volts, smart guy. Study hard."

"Sure, Pop," I said.

He wasn't aware that I hadn't been to a class in weeks, though exams were less than a month away. He hadn't seen the warning letter that had arrived with my dismal grades at the end of the fall semester.

I watched him through the chain-link fencing as he began to climb a steel staircase that took him up into a cloud of steam, and in a moment I could no longer see the stairs under his feet, only my father in his hard hat and coveralls, rising through the mist.

As I pulled out of the parking lot, the pigeons were already settling on the pipes overhead. I drove straight to Six-Mile Creek and the chubs.

Six-Mile may have had some natural beauty once. I don't know. By the time I discovered it that year, it had been trenched out and channeled around the new apartments and condos springing up along River Road. For most of its length, it was just a ditch really. There were chubs in every part of it.

At the mouth, where it emptied into the Niagara River, I could see their dark, cigar shapes filing past by the hundreds. Under the docks, where it had been dredged out for the boat basin, they cruised around the wooden pilings like cutouts on a spinning mobile.

I always fished upstream, away from the construction noise from the new subdivision. There was one natural bend left in the creek where a stand of sumac and wild grape had been spared the bulldozer's blade. The bushes crowded the bank and were taller than a man, and standing among them, I couldn't see the apartments or the boat basin, just a wall of vines and new budding leaves and the creek swirling below it, high and cloudy with runoff from the parking lots and freshly planted lawns.

There in the thicket, I felt like I was on a real stream, and I cast to those chubs as though they were wild mountain trout. Sometimes I would catch and release them all day, the hours racing by until it was time to pick up my father at the plant. But there were also times when the chubs were as finicky as game fish, slurping the real moths and ants off the surface, while refusing every imitation I offered. Then, when my best patterns drifted untouched, my mind would start to wander. I would begin to notice the sounds of the framing carpenters just beyond the bushes. I would begin to see the factory haze drifting over the big river and the rooftops of the apartments. And I would become keenly aware that a few miles away my chemistry class was just starting, or maybe calculus was ending, or that, if I left at that second, I could still make ROTC that afternoon.

I would think about a girl in English 110. Her name was Wendy, and she wore army fatigues and had the straight blond hair and pouty lips all the girls from the radical dorm seemed to have been born with. I used to sit near her and plan our camping trips to the Rockies, Yellowstone, the Sierra. She would bask nude in the sun while I fished high-country streams for cutthroats and rainbows. Still nude, she would cook over a small fire, the smoke clinging to her skin and to her hair for hours afterward. It should go without saying that we'd spend a lot of time in the sleeping bag.

I thought about our English instructor, Jeremy Stone, a graduate student and self-described "political anarchist." I wasn't sure what that meant but had a vague idea that bombs were involved; he looked capable of that with his wild black curls and matching beard. He drove a Harley to school, wore leather pants and the same black turtleneck for weeks at a time, a sweater with a hole under one arm that winked open and closed like the white mouth of a chub as he gestured wildly before the class. He looked like a guy who hadn't fished a day in his life, and Wendy never took her eyes off him.

No one with any common sense or pride fished for chubs, of course, so I almost always had Six-Mile to myself, though one day as I was walking back to the car, I was surprised to find a man wearing a gray jumpsuit with a Chevy emblem across the back sitting on a galvanized minnow bucket, still-fishing in the boat basin from a grassy bank opposite the docks. He was obviously a line worker from the GM plant up River Road, and sitting like that in his uniform, with his bait rod propped up in a forked stick at his feet, it looked like fishing was his job.

I don't know what he thought he was doing there with live bait. The only fish in the creek were the chubs, and they were hardly larger than minnows themselves. He may have heard something about pike running there. People were always starting such stories about some little ditch or pond or swamp in the county. There was never any truth to them. I think he was just killing time before punching in for the afternoon shift, because he stood and began reeling in just as I arrived. When he set down his rod and stooped to pick up his bait bucket, the gulls in the marina swooped down from every light pole and piling. They hovered above him, screaming and jockeying for position. He glanced up at them, took the lid off the pail, and heaved the contents straight up into the air. The bait water geyser rose and hung there a second, the minnows glittering in the afternoon sun, the gulls, wild now, spinning into them in a blur of white feathers. Then the whole thing collapsed. The water and the bait and the birds crashed into the basin, and the air was empty again. The fisherman picked up his tackle and headed back to the parking lot.

After he had driven off, I went down to the bank where he'd been fishing. I set my rod in his forked stick and sat on the grass, watching a lone gull swimming in a tight circle in the middle of the basin, its head cocked to one side, convinced there was still something good to be found there. I noticed that I could look out the mouth of the creek and down the big river and see the Chevy plant, and I was appalled. I swore that my life would never revolve in such a grubby little orbit, that my future would be different, special somehow. I think I believed that.

Each afternoon, when it was time to leave, I would take my rod down and hide it in the trunk, stash my fly box, wipe the creek mud from my shoes with a rag, and put that in the trunk too. Then I'd pick up my father and tell him, yes, everything was going fine at school, and no, I hadn't had time to apply for the jobs at the plant. And that's the way it went for the last month of the semester and into exam week, though toward the end, my father quit talking about the summer jobs, and about school, and finally grew silent altogether.

On days when I had no classes and no car, I slept late and spent the afternoons tying flies or just sitting on the porch listening to the radio. The Beatles were still big that year, and the Byrds, the Yardbirds, the Kinks, and the Stones. My little brothers were in school, and my mother was working a few afternoons a week at the front desk at the Holiday Inn. I had the whole house to myself, the whole empty neighborhood, and it seemed that it would go on forever like that. And then suddenly the semester was ending, and I was seized with the feeling that I had to get busy and do something.

The night before my last scheduled exam I was sitting at my desk, studying the Herter's catalog with its ads for rod-building kits, fly-tying thread, and hooks by the gross, when my father came into the room.

"You eat?" he said.

I told him I had eaten.

He sat against the edge of my desk next to a stack of outdoor magazines. He picked one up, thumbed through it. I watched him peer at the photos, reading each caption carefully. I realized that I had never seen him read anything but a newspaper, that he had no hobbies or interests I could name, that when he wasn't working he was doing chores around the house or yard or helping my mother with the little kids. He closed the magazine and held it on his lap. He seemed to be thinking about what he had read, and I wondered what he'd found in there that puzzled him so. Then he leaned forward and pulled back the window shade a bit and looked out at the street.

"Pretty quiet," he said.

"There's nobody left."

I meant the guys my age: Jimmy Augustino and Cosmo Poretti had joined the army right out of school and were somewhere in Vietnam. Johnny Ruswicki was in disc jockey school in Minnesota and trying to convince the draft board it was real college. Keith Sweeney had died of an overdose, and Joe Spano was in prison for helping fix the needle in Keith's arm. The younger guys, our little brothers, didn't live out on the street the way we had. Where were the whiffle ball games? The home run derbies? These kids didn't seem to exert the kind of presence we had on the neighborhood. Maybe it was the TV. People were just beginning to blame it for everything. Maybe they were right. In the next room I could hear the hum of the set, my brothers laughing at *Andy of Mayberry* or *The Beverly Hillbillies*.

My father let the window shade fall back into place.

"I take it you're not coming into the plant this summer."

I told him that the Rigi brothers were talking about painting houses. "I think they have some jobs lined up."

"Painting." He nodded. "I see." He stared at my unopened school books, but I couldn't read anything on his face except the exhaustion that was always there on work nights. Finally he said, "You're not coming into the plant because you're not going back to school in the fall. Am I right?"

"I don't know," I said. I was stunned that he knew how badly I was doing.

"And you don't much care for the army?"

He said that as though he just wanted to get the facts straight. Like he was taking notes on a curious life outside his own.

"I have some time. I'll go to Community in the fall, get the grades up, apply again for next spring." I heard myself saying that, and it sounded reasonable, but *fall* and *spring* were just words for things too far away to have any meaning.

"You understand I got no need for you to work at Hooker?" he said. "Maybe painting's a good thing for now. It's outside, at least."

It occurred to me that he was acting now, sparing me any further embarrassment. I didn't know whether to be grateful or furious.

"Sure," I said. "I'm going to be all right."

"Sure." He couldn't keep the sarcasm out of that, and I felt my face burn, but I held my tongue as he sat there quietly. After a while he said, "Something happened at the plant today." He looked at me, but I waited. "An accident," he said. "Guy named Seekins. One of the rebs. From Alabama, I think. I didn't know him well."

"Chlorine?" I remembered the day we got the news about my father. My mother bundling us up and into a cab for the trip to the hospital. I remembered my father in the big white bed, with tubes in his nose. I was so afraid of those tubes, and angry with him too. How could he lie still and let them do that to him? I remembered the coughing fits he had for days afterward, the way he would gulp a glass of ginger ale and then burp a tremendous, booming burp that left the whole room smelling like bleach.

"No," he said. "He stepped off the loading dock and hit his head on the truck. Fell maybe three, four feet."

"Dead?" I knew the answer already.

"Yeah, dead," he said, and it sounded like it was my fault somehow. Maybe he was just angry I had made him say it. "Very, very dead," he said quietly.

He stood to leave. He still had the magazine in one hand, and he flipped it open to the page he had marked with his thumb. There was a photo of one of the great sportsmen of the day, Lee Wulff maybe, or A. J. McClane. The man was holding a huge Atlantic salmon upside down by the tail, smiling broadly into the camera. My father held it up for me to see.

"Fishing," he said. "Grown men? I don't get it."

I almost started to say something, but it was clear he was not about to sit still for any lecture on the merits of fishing. Not from me. Not just then.

"I'm just saying, I don't get it," he said. He set the magazine down and walked out of my room.

I sat at my desk for some time, listening to the sounds of the house shutting down: my father wishing my mother good night as he turned in first, my brothers going off to their room when their show ended. A little later my mother knocked lightly on my door, three soft raps that were her way of saying good night without disturbing my studies. Then the house was quiet.

I wished my mother had come in. I wished she had come in and said something. I wished my father had said something more, something definite or demanding that would have made clear to me what I should do next. But the house was silent.

After a while I went to the kitchen, dark but for the small bulb in the range hood that threw a weak glow across the kitchen counters. My father would be the first one up in the morning, and my mother had his thermos standing ready by the electric coffeepot. On the kitchen table, my brother's school project, a salt and flour map of New York State, looked like a deformed pizza. I stared at the lumpy Adirondack and Catskill mountain ranges, at Lake Champlain painted in bright blue poster paint—beautiful places in my own state I had never seen. I took the car keys from the hook by the door and went out.

I drove to Pine Bowl. Bowling was out of favor with guys my age, but besides the alleys, Pine Bowl had a sizable billiards room. In the middle of the night, that's where I could always find one or two friends who had managed so far to avoid both the army and steady work.

The drinking age was eighteen then, and I ordered a beer and turned to find an old friend, Frank Machek, standing at the bar next to me. Frank used to live in the neighborhood when we were in grade school. We played down at the river at the end of the street, spearing carp in the warm green water near the sewage pipes, stoning the wharf rats, building trash fires. We'd take willow sticks and retrieve the rubbers that floated in the backwaters and boat slips like strange white eels. We called them Tonawanda whitefish and burned them in our fires, along with all kinds of flotsam: snarls of fishing line, bits and pieces of Styrofoam, plastic bottles and jugs. Frank taught me to do "pickle-on-a-platter" when the girls came down where we were skinny-dipping. He showed me how to burn the leeches off my ankles with an eight-penny nail heated to glowing in the fire. I thought we'd be friends forever.

Then, in eighth grade, he moved to another part of town, another school, and I lost track of him. Now he was wearing his hair down over his ears and had grown a sickly Fu Manchu mustache, and I kept studying him to find the old Frank I'd grown up with. He said he'd spent the last year traveling to Mexico "on business." I steered the talk to fishing, and he told me about trout streams in Colorado and New Mexico where the water was so clear the fish seemed to be suspended in air, and then I could see him again as I'd known him, with his flattop and his water-logged Keds. We had a few beers, and he revealed that he was on probation for a pot bust and would not be leaving town again soon. So I told him about the chubs, how easy they were to catch. I asked him to join me.

"No can do," he said. "I start at Bell tomorrow." He winked. "Look good for the court."

I tried to imagine Frank working an eight-hour shift at the huge aerospace plant on the edge of town. I tried to imagine anybody my age doing that.

I said, "Frank, they're going to give you a two-inch brush and a pot of glue, and you'll be sticking canvas to chopper blades till your back cracks. What kind of life is that?"

"A life," Frank said. He laughed. "A fucking life? I'm supposed to listen to that from a guy who fishes for chubs?" He walked off, shaking his head.

I finished my beer and tried to sort it all out because I have always been one to try to sort things out after a few beers—though it never comes to much. Frank Machek on the assembly line, Cosmo and Jimmy in Asia, Keith in his grave, and Joe in prison, the death of that guy Seekins at Hooker, a man I'd never even met. What did any of it have to do with me?

I walked out of Pine Bowl into a dense, black fog. One of the graphite plants was pulling a night discharge, something they did (then denied) all the time. In the swirling carbon dust, the big parking lot lights looked liked twenty-watt bulbs. The moon was lost in the black sky. A layer of fine soot covered my father's car. I ran the wipers and the windshield washers all the way home, hunched over the wheel and squinting through the smudged glass.

———

The next morning my father acted as though I was dropping him off at work and going to school as usual, as if he believed I was really planning to take my exam. We didn't talk much, and when we did we confined it to the haze hanging over the city. It was late May, hot and humid, and the black carbon dust stuck to everything. It clogged my nostrils and built up in the corners of my eyes. People were sweeping their sidewalks, hosing down their driveways. The little Italian man who owned the motel across from Great Lakes Carbon was out by the swimming pool trying to skim the black film off the surface with a push broom.

When I pulled into the parking lot at Hooker, my father didn't make a move for the door handle. He looked up at the factory looming before us: the tall wire fences and brick walls, the crisscrossed maze of rusted steel beams, the steam lines and gas lines and power lines snaking through the plant like tangled arteries and veins—everything leaking and dripping and crusted. For a long moment he sat and stared at it as if he'd expected to find something different there that morning. Then he turned to me.

"Let's go," he said.

"Go?"

He nodded. "You've got the light." He pointed to the traffic signal and waved me forward with one hand. I pulled back out onto Buffalo Avenue, mystified.

"Where are we going?"

"You pick. I'm with you." He leaned back into the seat, put his feet up on his hard hat.

I said, "Pop, come on. Really. What about your job?"

"Stop at the Texaco. I'll call in."

"You're taking the day off?" I felt the hairs on my arms standing up.

He shrugged. "I need a break."

"What are you going to do?"

"Let's do whatever you do all day. You know, a typical day, say."

The big vein in my neck began to pound. "A typical day?"

"Now you got it."

The entrance to the Thruway was approaching on the right. I put the turn signal on. "Typical?"

"Typical," my father said, and I turned onto the ramp and toward Six-Mile Creek.

That far from the factories the sky was still blue. Although technically it was spring, it was warm, and the summery odor of outboard gas was in the air. There were a dozen boats moored in the marina: cabin cruisers and smaller skiffs. An oily rainbow shimmered on the surface of the water around the docks. In the middle of the boat basin, a huge flock of bright white gulls bobbed in a raft.

"This is it?" my father said. His look seemed to say he had expected a little more.

"I guess so." I put my rod together and headed for the creek, wondering when he was going to put an end to this. But he just fell in behind me, and there was nothing I could do then but keep going.

The air was alive with mosquitoes, midges, and gnats as we walked along to my place in the sumac thicket. Brown and yellow grasshoppers catapulted from weed stems before us. I watched the chubs rising in the shallows, their fat gray bodies spiraling up to the surface like little missiles. My father made his way beside me, taking in everything but saying nothing. When we got to my spot, he took a seat on a tussock of new grass, folded his arms, and waited. And so I fished.

The chubs were feeding like never before, and they hit nearly every cast, no matter where it fell. Sometimes two, even three fish would streak toward the fly. If one spit the hook, another would devour it before I could retrieve. At times they struck while it was still in the air, inches above the surface.

I poured myself into it, forgetting the summer ahead and whatever came after that in the fall, forgetting my father behind me sitting in his coveralls and work boots watching me move up and down the bank taking chubs from behind every rock and midstream obstruction. I caught six in six casts behind a sunken lawn mower, three in a row out of the middle of a tire. I had never done anything so well in my life, and it was exhilarating. But after an hour or so the weight of his eyes on my back was too much for me, and I reeled in.

"We need to talk," I said.

My father said, "Keep fishing. They're really biting, aren't they? What are they, bass? Some kind of bass?"

I studied him to see if he was joking, but he was not. "No," I said. "Not bass. Listen, Dad—"

He waved me off. "Go on," he said. "I'll tell you when to stop." He shooed me back toward the creek with the backs of both hands.

I looked at him for a minute, and then I went back to fishing.

I fished right through that day, not even pausing to eat, although my father went back to the car around noon and brought his lunch pail down and sat munching his sandwiches behind me as I continued to cast. I didn't know how long he intended to pursue this, but with or without food I would last as long as he did, and I was ready to keep on until dark, or maybe until the creek dried up that summer, or until it froze again the following fall if I had to.

But when the action started to slow sometime in the late afternoon, and the fly floated a dozen drifts without a rise, I knew it was over, and I turned away from the water, about to admit that I had had enough, ready to move on to whatever came next between him and me. I found my father lying on his side in the sunny grass resting his head on one arm and snoring softly. I walked up and stood over him. His face looked gray and dry next to the moist new grass, the skin on his hands cracked and red. He had shaved that morning, but his cheeks were sharp with gray stubble again now and he looked so terribly old that I turned away, feeling I'd looked upon something I was not supposed to see.

When I looked back, a small blue moth had landed on the rim of my father's ear. It was a startling, chalky blue—not only its powdery wings, but its body, its legs, and its head. Even its twitching antennae were fine blue feathers. I found myself staring at the rhythmic flexing of its wings. While I watched, another identical moth landed within an inch of the first. An instant later a third and fourth joined them, and others clustered in the air around my father's head. I looked up to see that hundreds, maybe thousands, were now fluttering around us and just above the creek, their fierce blueness almost iridescent against the cracked mud banks.

Upstream and down, the moths continued to arrive, hard to see at first against the sky, then suddenly visible as they dropped low and hovered in a fluttering cloud inches above the water. In minutes the creek was covered with them and seemed to run as blue as the rivers of my dreams. I thought the chubs would materialize and tear into them, but nothing broke the surface, and the moths slowly began to lift off untouched. I watched them rise, not scattering across the fields the way they had come, but hanging together now like a flat blue ribbon that streamed upward and over the bushes and then the rooftops of the apartments, and finally disappeared into the blueness of the sky. I was still looking up at the empty air when my father awoke.

He squinted up at me. "You done?"

"I think so," I said. "I think I am."

He sat up and looked at the creek for a moment. "OK, then," he said. "Give me a hand up."

We walked back down to the car in silence again. Clouds were banking up over Canada just across the river, and when a shadow passed over us I was hit with a wave of late-afternoon sadness I would know again and again throughout my life. I loaded my stuff into the trunk and looked up to find my father peering toward the city so intently I had to look in that direction too. Even after he had turned away and gotten into the car, I remained staring.

From that distance I could just make out the tops of the smokestacks and cooling towers over the factories, and high above them the remains of the graphite cloud, a thin layer of black then hovering over the plants as though someone had taken a pencil and drawn a line across the sky to separate the pure summer blue from everything that lay below it.

But what I could not see was myself there among them ten years down the road with a wife and children and none of the skills needed to support us. What I couldn't see were the layoffs and cutbacks and plant closings, the lines at the unemployment office stretching down Pine

Avenue and around the corner, the past-due bills, the loans unpaid, the credit cards full and the checkbook empty. What I couldn't see was the journey back and forth across the continent in search of work, and a marriage collapsing as love gave way to shame and blame and the sure death of affection that goes with that whole life. What I couldn't see was me going to my father with my hand out like a beggar, like a stranger in need.

It was all out there in front of me, but as I got into the car, all I saw were the chubs rising again in the boat basin, their mouths blossoming like white flowers.

———————

Looking back now, after all this time, it's hard to believe that that's all there was to it, that my father and I didn't talk about anything of importance on the way home from the creek, didn't discuss what I had done or was going to do. Or not do. And if my failures disappointed him or hurt him, he didn't let on. I waited for days, for weeks. I waited for years. But he never mentioned it again, and I took his silence to mean that my life was mine to do with as I pleased. And so that's what I did.

What else was I to think? I was young. I was so young.

Things Come to Mind

M y wife walked into the kitchen and made the announcement: "We can't go to your folks' for dinner."

I was at the sink doing a few dishes. All I could do was look at her. I really thought she'd make it this time.

"I don't have any panty hose," she said.

She was still in her robe, though it was noon and we were supposed to be at my parents' shortly. The kids had been dressed for over an hour. They were starting to unravel.

She took a seat at the kitchen table, pouting. You could cut yourself on the corners of her mouth.

No panty hose. That was a new one. But was it reason enough?

I couldn't think about it. I really had to avoid that. The thought of breaking the news to my parents had to be pushed aside.

That seemed a bit risky. Pushing aside a thought.

I mean, what if nothing came to take its place?

Not to worry. Things come to mind.

Sometimes they relate directly.

Back when my wife and I first started having conversations like those, I went to see my father. He said, "Charlie, you expect too much, but you require too little. Too little." Then he rushed to add, "Not that a wife shouldn't come first. That's not what I'm saying, you understand?"

I said, "Yes." But, really, what else could I say?

Sometimes not so directly.

My father's left foot is two sizes larger than his right. It's a lot wider. You see what I mean?

All his life he's had to buy shoes from a special catalog. When I was a kid I loved to imagine the feet that went into the more exotic models pictured in it. Shoes for club feet, for crooked feet, for hopelessly flat feet, toeless feet, twisted feet, bent feet. Odd, nonmatching pairs—one perfectly normal, one grotesque.

The catalog even offered single shoes. You only had to specify L or R. I was glad for Mr. Manelli, across the street. He'd had one foot pinched off when a train wheel he was trying to grease lurched ahead.

When Mr. Manelli got out of the hospital, the railroad gave him a riding lawn mower. They gave his son Dominick a job for life. Very generous, considering that it was really only the company's policy to do that for families of the men actually *killed* on the job. Dominick immediately got married and moved his new wife into the house with his parents.

That's the way it is. Some things move when you least expect them, others won't budge at all.

It occurred to my wife that I was drifting off.

"Did you hear me? I can't go without hose."

She sat at the table, biting her nails. I took the seat across from her. I noticed how thin she was. That used to be a plus.

"It's Easter. Where are you going to find panty hose on Easter Sunday in this town?" I asked.

"I'm not," she said.

Unsolvable problems were sort of her hobby. That's one of those things you don't tell someone until after you're married.

"So, go without," I tried. "How about pants?"

"And look like a fool?"

"Nobody in my family is going to care."

"You got that right. Not about me they won't."

I had walked right into that one.

"Your brothers'll be there," she said. "Their kids. Your sister and hers. No shortage of people there."

We looked at each other for a minute, both temporarily out of ammo. I started drumming my nails on the Formica. Felt myself losing interest again.

Here's something.

One Saturday afternoon when I was a kid, I found my father sitting slumped over his knees on the front steps. He had his huge black accordion case on the porch above him. It looked bigger than him. Across the street, Mr. Manelli struggled to control the big lawn mower, as if that were his job. He crashed into the hedge again and again.

My father was wearing his suit—dark blue, with polished knees and elbows, dandruff on the shoulders. He had a wedding to play, but he was just sitting there on the steps, head down. I thought he was crying.

"Are you OK, Dad?"

He looked up at me, and I was glad to see there were no tears on his face. His eyes were darker than usual, though, the hollows circled in skin as dark as the graphite under his nails from the factory.

In the house, both my little brothers were crying. They'd started sometime the night before and had been at it almost all day.

"I gotta go to work, Chooch. I'm tired, is all."

He glanced at his watch and put his forehead back down on his knees, studying his big left shoe. There was a crack along one seam that showed a little sock. For months he'd talked about getting a new pair. But there'd been a lot of expenses lately—medical things. Measles, mumps, a variety of fevers that burned up every dollar, even with the side jobs, playing.

"Don't look so serious," he said. "This is shoe money today."

"Great, Dad," I said.

He stood and lugged the accordion case to the station wagon and wrestled it into the back.

"Help your mother if you can, Chooch," he said as he drove off.

"Well, I can see you don't care about my problems," my wife said. She stalked off to the living room, where the kids were still ripping through their Easter baskets.

I knew she wanted me to ask what she had done with the extra money I brought in last week.

I wasn't ready for that.

The fall before, she had said the girls needed back-to-school things, so I painted my boss's garage for cash. My wife took the girls to the mall, and they bought lunch boxes, pencil boxes, plastic notebook covers, and some other things I'd never seen before. They had lunch, saw a movie, bought some videos. Their school clothes went on the Sears bill.

I said, "Well, at least you had a nice time."

She said, "Shopping with children?"

The next job I did went to rent Halloween costumes. Sixty bucks to turn my children into two small space creatures. I said, "My mother used to make us costumes." My wife didn't speak for days.

I don't even want to talk about Christmas.

No. I knew better than to ask about the money.

Finally she yelled from the living room,"Easter candy costs plenty."

I couldn't argue with that. Candy is nice.

Even so, there were chocolate animals loose all over the house. Chocolate rabbits, chocolate chickens, chocolate ducks. There were marshmallow eggs. Baskets of jelly beans. Bushels of plastic grass.

"Plenty," she said again, more quietly.

What could I say to that? Don't ever do a nice thing for the kids again? Let the little monsters suffer?

I don't think so.

Certainly not on Easter.

"I'm going to paint Mrs. O'Sulivan's porch next weekend. We'll have a little extra," I told her through the wall.

"Don't forget Carla's communion," came back. "She'll be needing things."

"Shoes, I bet," I muttered to myself.

My dad and I loved to browse the shoe stores, as if they might somehow have a pair that would fit him. Fat chance.

He'd take a seat and pick up a display shoe—a sleek, black wingtip usually—cradling it in his hands like a baby. I'd sit next to him, dizzy from the smell of leather, shoe polish, and stocking feet.

When the clerk knelt before us, my father would push aside the sliding ruler and say, "No need to measure. What's the widest these come in?"

Whatever the clerk said, my father answered, "Perfect. Bring me a pair in a ten and a half. A man should know his own shoe size, right, Charlie?"

"Right, Dad."

By the time the clerk returned, my father would already be down to his socks, the shoe horn in one hand.

He'd slip his right foot in. The left one wasn't so easy, but he'd force it somehow. Sometimes I could see the knuckles of his toes through the leather.

Then he'd walk back and forth before the full-length mirror, drinking in the picture of himself in shoes he would never own.

After a minute he'd limp back to the chair.

"They seem a little tight," he'd say, looking surprised.

I'd shake my head at the clerk, letting him know just how disappointed my father and I were in him.

The poor guy. He was only trying to do his job.

I had to stop daydreaming for a minute. It was time to assign blame.

"If you hadn't had the truck all day yesterday, I might have got some panty hose."

She was serious.

I could've pointed out that Easter Sunday isn't a surprise holiday, that there is plenty of advance notice from the Hallmark people and others, that, with the help of certain almanacs, a person could actually determine the dates for the next several thousand years.

Somehow I didn't think that was the best strategy.

"I was working yesterday," I said.

I heard her rustling around on the couch in the living room.

"You take the kids and go," she said. "Nobody'll miss me. Not your mother or father."

Me and the kids alone? For some reason, that would be even harder to explain. And then there was the thought of my wife sitting home all afternoon, alone, surrounded by chocolate animals. That could cost me plenty in the long run.

"No," I said. "I'll call and tell them we're not coming."

A little more pain wouldn't kill my parents. Only, why did *I* have to be the one to dish it out?

This came up about pain.

My dad came home from playing a wedding one Saturday night with his special left shoe sticking out of his suit coat pocket. It had a long split down one seam. The sole was flapping loose.

I'd seen him come through that door hundreds of times—dirty from the factory or tired from hours on stage with the accordion in his arms— but I'd never seen him come home with one shoe off.

He just stood in the doorway holding the accordion case in his left hand, his wide stocking foot flattening out under the weight, a bewildered look on his face that seemed to say, "How did I get here? How did I ever get to this particular place in my life?"

My mother looked at the ruined shoe. She said, "Anthony, why'd you wait so long?" She bit one knuckle and made her saddest face.

My father didn't say a word. He left the accordion case in the hallway and went down into the cellar. Didn't even take off his suit coat.

"Anthony," my mother called after him.

But he didn't come back up for fifteen minutes, and she didn't go downstairs. When he finally reappeared in the kitchen, he was wearing his shoe again. It was completely wrapped in silver duct tape.

"I think it'll hold through mass," he said, and headed off to the bedroom.

Every step he took, the shoe squeaked.

"I better go talk," my mother said to me.

She kissed me good night, squeezed past the accordion case and down the hall. I went to bed.

Just before dawn, the whole house shook. I thought Khrushchev had finally flipped his lid and dropped the big one on us.

My mother had gotten up to use the bathroom and smashed her foot into the heavy case in the dark hallway.

She sat on the accordion and howled.

When we got to her, her right baby toe was sticking straight out sideways. The whole special shoe catalog flashed across my mind.

She cried, "Anthony, I wish you didn't have to work so much."

———————

It was really getting late. My parents were going to be wondering what had happened to us.

I went to the living room and stepped over the kids to get into my Lazy Boy. "Angela, honey," I said to my little one. "Be careful. You're getting chocolate on Carla's dress."

My wife was lying on her side on the couch. She had her legs pulled up under her robe, and it looked like she had no feet.

"What am I going to tell my folks?" I said.

"The truth."

The last time it was "the car won't start." Before that, "I have to work." They understood those well enough. Or they acted like they did.

"How come you don't want to go anywhere?" I said to my wife.

"Don't say that about me! I want to go plenty of places. There's a whole world of places out there I'd like to go to. There's a Disneyland in Florida now. I don't see us going there."

She said "in Florida now," as if the new Disneyland was so much closer to New York than the one in California that we might walk right over.

"Don't you say that," she said. "The girls would just love to go someplace like that."

I reached for the phone on the coffee table. I dialed my parents' familiar number without thinking about it.

Not that I wasn't thinking at all, mind you.

The morning my mother separated her toe, our whole family went to church directly from the emergency room. My mother wore a bedroom slipper over her bandaged foot. My father was in his blue suit and wounded shoe.

We were late. The Pakistani intern had been slow in filling out the report. There'd been some difficulty explaining the part the accordion had played in it all.

We had to take the back-row pew because Father Berrano ran the mass like an opera—latecomers were discouraged from wandering in once the performance had started. I must say, his *Dominus vobiscums* were worth it.

When the time came, my father offered his shiny elbow to my mother, and she limped along beside him to the communion rail. I stayed in the pew with my sister and the little ones.

My parents were moving slowly. Before they were halfway back to our row, most people were already back on their kneelers, sucking communion wafer out of their teeth. Even Mr. Manelli had hopped back and put up his crutches on the seat beside him.

My father kept a slow pace for my mother. They smiled through the sacrament's afterglow. Maybe that was just the light through the stained glass.

Mass was crowded, as it often was in those days, but it was quiet. In the silent church, the silver-taped shoe squeaked louder than ever. My mother's slipper flapped against the hard marble floor.

People started to look up from their missals, their rosaries. Even Father Berrano waited to begin the benediction. I swear the statues turned to catch a glimpse of them passing, arm in arm, flapping and squeaking down the aisle, beaming like saints. A mother of four limping to communion on a broken toe, a man with one pair of dress shoes and a roll of tape.

To this day, I'm sure that had we been a more demonstrative religion, say, Baptists, the whole room would have erupted in applause.

"What are you smiling about?" my wife asked.

I held the phone to my ear, waiting for my parents to answer.

"Just thinking about something."

"What?"

"Hello, Dad? It's me, listen we uh—"

"I really can't go," my wife said. "Do you understand that?"

"Hold on a minute, Dad."

I covered the phone.

Little Angela had draped plastic Easter grass over my wife's head and stuffed a doll into the front of her robe. Only the doll's head stuck out, under my wife's chin. My wife had closed her eyes at this and had drawn her knees all the way up to her chest.

In a barely audible voice she said, "Tell them we're coming down with something."

At the moment there was nothing cluttering my mind.

I could see that she was absolutely right.

Raccoon

R andy wanted to hunt, and there was no talking him out of it,
although the temperature was down in the teens again after a week
of thaw and drizzle, the roads so slick I wasn't even going to try to make
the bar scene for a change. He was home on leave after basic training and
phoned on a Saturday night, the first week in January. This was 1968, and
we were not yet twenty years old.

"Hunt what?" I pinned the phone against my ear and pulled back the
drapes. In the glistening pavement, every porch lamp, every lighted window on the block glowed double like an upside down neighborhood. "It
looks like somebody ran a Zamboni down the street."

"It could be the last time we get to do this," he said. There was a cool
distance to his voice, and I could see where friendship might be taking
a back seat for a while in any case: On Monday, Randy was leaving for
California and then on to Vietnam. I was not going. Not then, not ever. I
hoped that was all there was to his frostiness, because the only other
problem we might have had was named Tina Bustamenti, and I didn't
even want to think about that.

I said, "OK. We can hunt, I guess. Sure."

"I'll pick you up in the morning," he said. "Seven thirty."

In the background I heard someone wailing. Female.

I said, "Is everything all right?"

She was sobbing now, choking on whatever was wrong between them.

Randy said, "I'll bring the dogs."

I heard something fall over and break: glass, a bottle maybe.

"Randy . . ." I said. But the wailing picked up again, and then the line went dead.

Tina B. She and Randy had been a couple since eleventh grade. I would have recognized that crying anywhere.

In the morning, Randy's hunting beater was waiting in my driveway when I opened the front door to check the still brutal weather. The sky was black, but in the porch light I could see tongues of exhaust whipping across the icy blacktop in the wind, and I got the weird feeling he'd been there a long time, waiting, watching the house. I waved and his lights came on.

I put my shotgun in the back with Randy's beagles, Moose and Lucy, and I got in the car. He looked at me and shook his head. "Nice hair," he said. "Remind me to do something like that with mine when it grows back. *If* I live that long."

I said, "Come on. It's bad luck to talk like that."

"Bad luck," he said to the windshield. "I'm five days from Vietnam, and he's talking about luck."

I didn't know what to say to that. We sat there in the driveway a minute longer listening to the wind moaning through the vents. One of the dogs groaned impatiently. The subject of Tina seemed to be squatting in the back seat behind us, ready to tap me on the shoulder. Being a coward, I was not about to turn and face it.

"Bad luck," he said. "Christ." He punched the radio on and headed out into the country.

The summer before, Randy had been out of town for a while, working on a road job with his father's paving company, and I was playing drums for a group at a local bar called Caniglio's. The band was from Cleveland, and something unfortunate had happened to their drummer—overdosed or got drafted or married or something—so I was filling in.

One night after the gig I gave the lead guitar a ride to his motel. He was a bone-skinny stoner, an older guy—maybe twenty-five or so—hip and weird in a phony, practiced way and continually wasted. That night he had downed a quart of vodka and a bottle of Robitussin with codeine and was in no condition to drive. His motel was a horrible little place across from the DuPont plant—burned-out sign, fake brick siding, windows opaque with whatever it was that hung in the air there. And when I pulled up outside his room the door opened, and there was Tina

Bustamenti in a T-shirt and white panties, leaning into the door frame with the telephone receiver wedged against her ear and a magazine open in her hands. She had her head down, looking at the magazine as she talked into the phone, and her long black hair fell over her face. She didn't even look up, just swung the door wide, turned her perfect keister to my headlights, and waltzed back inside.

On the drive out into the farm country, Randy stared out at the feeble winter dawn and barreled past snowed-over potato fields and rows of naked fruit trees shuddering in the driving wind. The sky was an icy metallic gray, and there was little moving on the land: one skittish fox fidgeting along the shoulder of the road; a flock of hen pheasants, paper-bag brown against the glazed snow, pecking at scraps of feed corn. Rabbit was the only game in season, and that's what we said we were hunting, though there was no reason to think they'd be out on a day so grim.

For the sake of conversation I said, "We should be ice fishing."

Randy frowned. "Sit over a hole and jerk your little rod up and down? I got enough of that in Basic."

"OK," I said. I was glad to have him talking again, but not too sure I liked where it was headed. Still, he wasn't letting it drop.

"How about you? I hear the hippie college chicks snap it up like licorice."

"Are you kidding me?" I said. "That place is a war zone. Protests, sit-ins. The girls are hot for the Movement guys, the guys with signs, with slogans. Those chicks wouldn't give a townie mouth to mouth if he was turning blue."

Randy was quiet again and seemed to be thinking about that as we turned into the driveway of a farm that had a fair-sized woodlot on the property. We slid to a stop in front of the house—chalky white clapboard and lots of crumbling gingerbread. The yard was a sheet of crystallized snow, and in the middle of it there was a statue of the Virgin Mary, wind-scarred and listing to one side as though she'd caught a stray bullet.

Randy got out and yanked the zipper of his hunting coat up to his chin. I noticed how huge he looked, how the army food had bulked him out. He leaned back into the car, and I thought he was reaching for something in the glove box in front of me until he stopped, knuckles pressed into the seat beside me, the brim of his cap actually touching my forehead.

"A 'war zone'?" he said. "Man, you're a riot today." He paused there a moment, searching my eyes for something before he drew back. "You better stay put. These farm folks get a load of that fag musician hair and we'll never get permission to hunt." He shook his head and muttered "war zone" and headed for the front door.

For the next cold, miserable hour or so we slid and slipped along a small creek bed, stopping to let Moose and Lucy work brush piles, thickets, anything big enough to hold a rabbit. There was no warmth in the low winter sun, and my toes were soon aching, my fingers dead. There was nothing moving except the ice-laden branches overhead and the bare brown vines that trailed from them. I was exhausted from post-holing through the crust, and I wondered what it had been about hunting that I used to love so much, that had kept me wide-eyed and tossing all night before the small-game opener every year since I was fourteen. Because whatever it had been was gone then, and all I could think about was the new band I was in and the club date we had coming up and so forth. None of which Randy wanted to hear about. Since we had left the farmhouse he had spoken only to his dogs. It was just as well.

———————

One night, earlier that winter, shortly after Randy had left for basic training, I had been between gigs and out for a good time at Caniglio's. It was "twenty-five-cent tequila night," and the place was mobbed. That was the year of the strobe light, the black light, the fog machine, the year of the fuzztone and the wawa pedal. That was the year we danced in a haze of patchouli and pot and said "Oh wow!" and meant it.

This particular night I worked my way through the swaying, grinding mob at Caniglio's and found myself snug up against a very drunk Tina Bustamenti. She was dancing with one of the Romecki sisters, holding her drink over her head, laughing, having a good time, and—as I said—totally blasted. Her hair looked like it had been whipped by demons, and she was wearing a sleeveless pink top that was so thin and tight you could read the laundry instructions on her bra. When she turned and saw me, her face went slack and she started with tears that could get your flood insurance canceled. She missed Randy, she shouted over the roar of the music.

"I miss him too," I yelled.

She said, "But *I* love him!"

Now her mascara was running down her cheeks in little black rivulets, and I got the feeling I was supposed to say or do something about that. But we were standing in front of amps designed for stadiums—a few more decibels and eardrums would start bleeding—and I was *not* about to scream, "I LOVE HIM TOO!" So I just nodded, and Tina stood there swaying like a weed, her eyes all over the room now, pupils dilated wide enough to park a truck in. It finally occurred to me that she was on a lot more than booze.

"Dance with me?" she shouted, and fell against my chest, basically unconscious.

Tina freaking B.

I helped her to the door and we sat in her car for an hour, waiting for her to drift down out of the ozone. There were more I-miss-Randys, and tears again, though now she was hanging on my neck and moving in ways that could not be misinterpreted. In some cranny of my pickled brain I saw Randy huffing through the obstacle course at Fort Bragg, carrying on his back the entire history of our childhood together, and I knew that I needed to get out of Tina's car right then. But Tina was wearing a skirt you could use for a headband, and I was operating with the kind of judgment that comes with two dollars worth of twenty-five-cent tequilas. Enough said.

In a while Randy's dogs brought us to a huge cottonwood tree, three feet or more in diameter and twisted and leaning at an impossible angle, but anchored into the ground with splayed root knees jutting out like buttresses. Moose began digging like a badger at a little cave under one of the roots, and in a minute he had his whole face in the hole. Lucy stood beside him, barking into his ear.

Randy seemed content to stand there watching the dogs, but I was cold and tired, and I couldn't take his silence another minute. We'd been together forever. I started kindergarten with this guy. First Communion. Confirmation—we took the same name: Peter (Jesus's fishing buddy). We had shared eight, maybe ten trout openers. Hunter safety training. All the biggies.

I finally started to say something—God only knows what—when Moose pitched back from the roots, howling and spraying a fountain of blood from his nose and muzzle. There was a blur of brown fur at the mouth of the hole and then something scrambling across the ice and careening off the smaller trees around the giant cottonwood. Lucy was right behind the creature, bawling madly, followed by Moose again, still bleeding and howling louder yet.

Randy swung his gun to his shoulder and drew down on the animal but lowered it again. "Raccoon," he said, as it skidded into the base of a small tree and scurried up the narrow trunk until it had pulled itself into the branches twenty feet above the howling, jumping dogs. Randy set his gun against a log, collared Moose, and held him between his knees to inspect the gashes on his muzzle. After a minute he looked up from the squirming dog and studied the raccoon. "It's a young one," he said. "Last year's kit." He stood, still holding Moose by the collar. He got still, kind of dreamy eyed, and I could see he was thinking about something, and I thought, oh boy, here it comes.

He turned to me. "I want it. I want you to keep it for me."

I looked up at the little animal perched on a branch, clinging to the tree trunk with its monkeylike hands. It curled its lips back and hissed, showing a mouthful of yellow teeth.

"Alive?"

"That's it," Randy said. "Alive."

I looked at Moose's bleeding nose, then up the tree again.

"Randy, I don't know."

"Yes you do," he said. "You know, all right. Until I get back."

"It's wild," I said.

He nodded. "One tour. One year." He gave me a look that said, is that so much to ask? I said nothing.

"Good," he said. He leashed the dogs and clipped them to a tree, shrugged off his coat, and stood there in his wool shirt tying the coat sleeves together to make a sack out of it. When he had it the way he wanted, he set the coat on the snow and pulled his gloves on. "Ready?"

I set my gun down, thinking that only a year or two before, nothing on this earth would have sounded like more fun than trying to catch a live raccoon, that I would've already been planning the cage I'd build and what I'd feed it. Now I was just cold and tired and wishing none of this had happened to us: this thing with Tina, this war. "I guess so," I said.

Randy got a grip on a vine dangling from the little tree and began yanking, putting his weight into it until the whole tree was rocking. The last of its dead leaves came loose and the wind ripped them away and they were gone, and the raccoon was hanging from the naked tree with one little hand, flapping like a flag. Randy kept yanking, and the tree whipped back and forth, and finally the raccoon came sailing down at our feet and we dove on it.

It got crazy then. The two of us sliding around on the glazed snow in a knot, arms and legs flailing. The little animal under us somewhere, and Randy taking everything out on it, and on me—thrashing like a wild man, punching and kicking. I caught an elbow to the nose and heard something snap and my face went numb and my stomach turned over and I lost track of the raccoon. Randy kept thrashing.

When he finally slumped to a stop, I was facedown against the frozen snow. I felt something move under my chest, and I closed my hand around a mass of warm fur and realized I had lost one glove in the melee. I squirmed out from under Randy and got to my feet, holding the hissing, twisting animal by the scruff of its neck.

"I got him!" I said, as the raccoon kicked and clawed and tried to swing its hind feet up and wrap them around my arm. I kept my elbow high and held the little beast out by my fingertips, keeping it as far from me as possible. The dogs were *really* going nuts now, howling, leaping high at the ends of their leashes, and crashing on the ice each time they landed. Randy picked himself up. He pulled a handful of snow and ice out of his shirt collar and looked at my face.

"Your nose is broke." It was not an apology.

I heard him through a buzzing hum that seemed to be coming from the middle of my face, and I knew he was right.

"Just get the coat before this thing grabs me," I said.

As Randy turned for the coat, the raccoon went limp in my hand and I could see its little eyes shifting around looking for an opening. I also saw that I had the skin of its neck pinched between three fingers and my thumb, and that my right pinky was sticking straight out next to its ear. But I was too late. It reached up, wrapped its hand around my finger, pulled it into its mouth and bit down with all its little raccoon might. The pain shot right up to my elbow.

Randy looked up from the coat as I screamed and shook the raccoon off my hand. It flew a couple of feet and ran up the long, sloping trunk of the giant cottonwood tree. There was a neat, deep puncture wound in the pad of my fingertip, a jagged hole on top where my nail was missing. A stream of dark blood erupted, brilliant red against the snow. The dogs continued howling. Randy grabbed my hand and pried the fingers open to look at the bite.

"How do you feel about rabies shots?"

"Rabies?"

I had visions of doctors hammering foot-long needles into my stomach. My finger was throbbing. My wrist and arm ached. I could feel my nose closing up, my face swelling. I tried to pull my hand away from Randy's grasp, but he clutched it, watching the blood puddle in my palm.

Still hanging on to my hand, Randy said, "While we're standing here doing nothing like this, let me tell you about last night."

I said, "I was going to . . ."

But his hand tightened around my wrist and he shot me a look like he might smash me in the nose again.

"Just listen to this, OK? Every day since I've been home from Basic, I've asked Tina to marry me. No dice. She's not ready, she says. Not ready. So yesterday I go, 'OK, let's give it a year then. I don't care what you do, who you do it with, but get it out of your system. And when I get back from 'Nam we get married. No questions asked. Deal?' All of a sudden I'm Saint Randy. I mean she can't believe how understanding I'm being. Like I haven't figured out that I can't expect her to just sit on that thing while I'm in Asia. So she goes on a confession jag you wouldn't believe, and I have to sit through the complete list. Names, places, how many times."

Randy let my bloody hand fall away, wiped his own on his pants, and picked up his shotgun. I packed my finger in snow that went red as fast as I could pile it on. "Look," I said, wanting to tell him before he told me that he knew.

But he shook his head and held up his hand. "Don't say one single word."

All there was between us then was the sound of the wind in the trees.

"This goes on forever with her," he said. "She's talking about guys I know, guys I never heard of. But I'm cool, and when she finally winds down we start getting close again and then wham, her eyes open up and she goes, 'There's one more.' I go, 'Tina, enough!' But she goes, 'No. You need to know about this one.'"

My face went hot.

He was facing me, the muzzle of his shotgun rising toward me. I watched until it was at gut level. And still it kept coming.

He was saying something. But I just stood there, deafened now by a pounding in my ears, and mesmerized by the perfect round, black opening of the gun barrel moving in a small circle less than a foot before me as he gestured with it. I had the oddest thoughts about the shot pattern, how tight it would be at that range: the entry hole would be no bigger than the muzzle, the exit probably the size of a fist, as the shot pulled a chunk of meat and bone along with it. I closed my eyes and waited for the tight wad of BBs to smash into me, through me. It will look like an accident, I thought. Happens all the time. But when I felt the thump against my chest I opened my eyes to find Randy jabbing me with the gun barrel, and my ears cleared and I heard the dogs whining in frustration at the ends of their leashes.

I have heard people say there are worse things than death, and maybe that's true, though at that moment, nothing could have made me believe it. Because I felt the wind on my face again and it felt good, and I felt the pain once again in my hand and in my nose and that was not good, but better than being dead by a long, long stretch.

I had no idea what Randy said or what I agreed to or admitted or, for that matter, if I spoke at all. Randy lowered the gun and looked away. He bent and picked up his coat. I stood there cradling my chewed-up hand in the other one, a headache building like a thunderstorm in my sinuses behind my smashed nose. With the threat of the gun gone, my mind shifted back to the thought of rabies.

I looked up at the raccoon. "Shoot it for me? They'll need its head. I can't handle the gun."

Randy glanced up the huge cottonwood. He said, "That animal's not rabid, college boy. He just woke up pissed, is all." He picked up my glove off the ice and handed it to me. "Put this on and try not to faint before we get back to the car. I don't want to have to carry you on this stuff."

He unleashed the dogs and picked up my gun for me, but before we started back he turned and said, "One thing I want to know."

I felt my heart stall.

He said, "You would have kept it for me, right?"

Without a second's hesitation I answered, "I would have kept it for you." And I heard it come out evenly, as though I really believed I had that kind of loyalty and honor in me somewhere.

Randy hesitated a beat and then smiled. "Sure," he said. "I knew you would." But as he was about to turn away I saw the cold shadow of truth pass over his eyes, and that is the face I will always remember him with.

The next time I saw Tina Bustamenti was that spring, at Randy's funeral. He was the first from our town to die in the war, and Amato's funeral parlor was jammed: relatives, the guys from the neighborhood, a military escort for the flag-draped coffin that held however much of him they had sent back from Asia. And Tina, of course, right down in front with Randy's mom and dad.

She was a wreck at the funeral. But she would recover. A year later she would marry Steve Pascuzzi of Pascuzzi Insurance. She and Steve would have two children and matching Mustangs—candy apple red. They would live in a four-bedroom Cape Cod in the best neighborhood in town for a short while, until they would divorce.

Time went by and the war dragged on and did not go well for either side, as near as I could figure. By then I had a wife and child too, and I never had to go. So I was still in town—not hunting anymore (I had given that up, finally) but still playing weekends to supplement the crap money I made painting houses. And from time to time I would see Tina in the bars, cruising for men, and starting to look a little too old for it, though still a knockout in a short skirt.

We were just friends then. And sometimes, when I was on a break, she and I would sit and have a beer and talk—about her kids, about mine, about anything but Randy. All around us there would be younger people, drinking and preening and posing, as people will in a club. And sitting there among them with Tina like that, I could see in their smiles, and hear in their laughter, that life felt to them the way it had to us during that time, our time, only a few years earlier, when, for a brief moment, I think we truly believed that we were getting away with something.

Sick Baby

————

His name was Tom, and it was his twenty-second birthday the after-noon he came home from deer hunting with his brother and his wife told him that their daughter was in the hospital.

Tom hadn't even gotten all the way into their apartment, a tiny two-bedroom flat on the second floor, above the home of an old Italian couple in the oldest neighborhood in town. He was still at the top of the stairs when she told him the baby was sick, still at the door to the apartment, still wearing his boots and his blaze-orange coat, the pockets heavy with deer slugs. He had his shotgun in one hand, his empty thermos in the other. He was hungry after the long drive home from the Southern Tier, and the oily aroma of Mrs. Cabucini's homemade sauce was wafting up the stairway from the house below, and he found his mouth filling with saliva. He was still in the doorway, which opened into their little kitchen, where his wife was now standing, her back against the counter near the sink, arms folded across her chest. She was wearing one of his sweaters, something he usually found appealing, sexy for some reason. But not today. Today it made her look heavy, a little wide. The kitchen was bright, the midafternoon sunlight glowing on the painted yellow walls, glisten-ing in the silver tubing of the chrome-legged table and chairs. The counter was clean, and there was no sign or smell of food. On the drive home from hunting, Tom had wondered if his wife would bake him a birthday cake, but there would be no cake now. How could there be? The baby was sick.

His wife said, "I didn't know what to do. I couldn't get a hold of you."

Tom put the thought of food aside. He tried to determine whether it was anger or fear he saw in his wife's eyes. Their daughter was not yet two years old and had been sick off and on for most of her short life. The doctors couldn't say what was wrong, and they kept testing her for increasingly more frightening diseases. In the past year they had begun mentioning the kinds of things that there were charitable organizations named after, things that aging, once-popular actresses raised money to combat. Nothing ever came of the tests. No one ever had an answer. Lately the child had been a little healthier, however. And earlier that month, when his wife had asked him what he wanted for his birthday, Tom had said, "I want to go hunting." And his wife had said,"You should go. You need a break. Go."

But now she just stood leaning against the counter and said, "You weren't here."

He had been gone three days. His boss at the paint store had also been a hunter once, in his youth, and he had given Tom the Friday off for his birthday. Tom and his brother, Sidney, rented a cabin in Allegheny State Park, a hundred miles south of the city, in the snowy, wooded hills near the border of Pennsylvania. There was no phone, no way to get a hold of him. That was the whole point.

His wife leaned farther back into the counter. She said, "She's in the hospital."

Tom had managed to enter the kitchen now, and as he stood there in the overheated air of the little room, the word *hospital* formed on his lips but went no further. They had been through so many times like this. How worried was he supposed to be? Who could tell him that?

He stepped out of his boots and slid them off to one side of the door. The boots looked huge there. There was so little space. One extra thing, and you were smothered. He set the big thermos beside them. He still had the shotgun in his other hand, and it felt tremendously heavy now.

"The hospital?" he said, finally. "What?"

Sidney had gone to the hospital in an ambulance one Christmas Eve when they were children. At the time, Tom was a teenager and his brother was seven or eight. He had a rare form of chickenpox that sent him into convulsions in the middle of the night. He was in a coma for days and barely conscious for weeks after that, his brain scrambled by the fever that had almost killed him. He got his Christmas presents more than a month later when he came home from the hospital at last and could think straight again. And the thing that Tom remembered most about the whole episode was the dreary, hollow event the opening of his brother's presents had been, how completely wrong and empty and cruel it had seemed to make Sidney do that on a sunny afternoon in February, when all the joy of Christmas was long over.

"What happened to her?" Tom said. "What's wrong with her now?"

His wife studied him a moment, then turned her back on him. She took a glass from the counter and filled it with tap water, drinking the whole thing in one long, slow swallow, as though she had been waiting for him to return before she could do anything—even drink water. While he waited for her answer, he laid his shotgun on the kitchen table.

She finished her water but didn't turn around. She was going to make him wait some more. Like he had made her wait for him to come home from hunting, and the baby was sick. He slipped off his coat and hung it over the back of the nearest chair, more comfortable now in his jeans and shirt and wool socks, but still too warm. Though he had closed the door behind him, the smell of Mrs. Cabucini's sauce was as strong as ever, like it was coming right up through the floor. But he wasn't thinking about food now and didn't notice that.

His wife still hadn't turned around. She still hadn't told him what was wrong with the baby. He thought about moving to her, touching her or putting his arm around her, but he could tell it was not the thing to do. So he waited, thinking about the fun he and his brother had had hunting. Was it worth it? Was it worth this?

It had snowed hard the day they got to the mountains, and the forest was a wonder of white-crowned pines and hardwoods. Nothing would move in the heavy, wet snow, and they hadn't seen a deer the whole weekend. But on Sunday morning, the sun finally emerged and flooded the world with dazzling white light. And while Tom stood in a tree stand at the edge of the forest waiting, he witnessed a black bear venture out into the blazing white field of new snow less than a hundred yards from where he was perched. It was the first wild bear he had ever seen and was even bigger than he had expected a bear to be, and blacker, so black it looked like negative space moving across the snow. He wanted to tell his wife about it, how fantastic it had been to see a wild bear in the snow like that, and on the way home he had thought about how best to capture the scene. But now he had to wait until she told him what was wrong with their daughter, who was sick and in the hospital. Because, of course, he couldn't talk about a bear now. Now he had to wait.

His wife finally turned from the sink and looked at him wearily. She was a year younger than Tom, though when she was tired like she was now, she looked much older than that.

"What's wrong with the baby?" he asked again. He tried to make himself sound more worried than he actually felt, because for some reason he was not as panicked as he felt he should be, and he kept finding himself reliving the hunting trip, which was so strongly planted in his mind right then that he could barely think about anything else.

How much fun it had been making their own meals on the gassy camp stove in the little cabin, playing gin rummy and drinking beer—not foolishly, recklessly like he had in high school, but easily, comfortably, like a grown man who had worked and earned the beer he was drinking and the food he was cooking and the time he spent hunting. He thought about the first night in the cabin, with the snow still coming down hard outside and the fire in the woodstove a glowing red ring around the stove door in the darkness. And how, as he was dozing off, almost asleep, he realized that it was the first time he had slept alone, without his wife, in the two years since she had spent a night in the hospital for the birth of the baby. And that he didn't miss her at all.

"There's nothing wrong with the baby," his wife said. She looked right into him.

He thought she meant that the doctors were mistaken about the baby's condition. He wasn't sure what she meant.

"She's better now?"

"She's fine," his wife said. "She's asleep in her room."

"At the hospital?" He still didn't get it.

His wife hung her head, shook it tiredly, and sighed. "She didn't go to the hospital. She's right here." She waved toward the narrow hallway that connected the kitchen with the tiny living room at the other end of the apartment. The bedrooms were on either side of the hall and had ceilings that sloped with the angle of the roof so that you could stand upright in only part of each room. Although one of the two rooms was decorated with Disney cartoon wallpaper and had every hanging toy ever manufactured dangling from the ceiling, until recently, the baby had spent most of her life sleeping across the hall in their bedroom, in her crib at the foot of their bed, so they could keep an eye on her.

"Here?" Tom said. He looked down the hall. There was a small plastic toy piano lying on its side on the carpet near the baby's bedroom door. There was a tiny yellow sock on the floor there too.

"Why did you say that about the hospital?" Tom said.

His wife looked at the shotgun on the kitchen table. She looked more tired than he had ever seen her, though it was midafternoon. She looked half asleep.

"Why?" he said, more curious than angry. He couldn't imagine a reason that made any sense, and it reminded him that at times he had no idea how his wife thought. No idea at all.

His wife looked from the gun to him. "I wanted to know if you had a good time hunting this weekend. I wanted to know if it was fun." She turned away and walked down the hall, past their daughter's room and toward the living room, stepping over the toy piano and the sock on the floor. Over her shoulder she said, "So, now I know."

The bear came across the field of brilliant white snow toward Tom as though it intended to climb right up the tree he was standing in. And then it stopped directly below him and looked up, as if Tom had made a sound, though he was sure he hadn't. The bear stared at him, and he stared at the bear. And for a long moment they studied each other under the bright winter sun—neither one of them having any way of knowing that this was going to be the most interesting thing that would ever happen to them.

All the while, Tom looked down the barrel of the gun and thought about shooting the bear, because after all, he *was* hunting; he had a license, and slugs that looked like they could stop a rhinoceros. But he didn't shoot because, really, what would you do with a dead bear? Mounts and rugs and skins on the wall were for hunters who could afford taxidermists, and that was not even something to dream about. And anyway, even if you could afford it, how would a bearskin look on the wall of an apartment hardly large enough to turn around in? You might think it was fine at first, exciting, adventurous in some way. But sooner or later, you would look at it hanging there, looming over the couch or the television set, all teeth and claws and black shaggy fur, and you would ask yourself, how did something like that ever get into our house? How?

Side Job

————

Franklin's dog was loose again.

The first time it had cost him fifty dollars. The second time it was seventy-five. The town took its leash laws seriously. They'd want a hundred this time around, and Franklin didn't have a hundred dollars to bail out a dog. He didn't have a hundred for anything just then.

His wife, Julie, gave him the news when he got home from the warehouse. "Suzy's at the Kwik Shop over on River Road," she said. "Or at least she was an hour ago. The Skidmore boy came by after school to say he'd seen her running with some kids there. I tried to call you at work, but you'd already left. Where've you been, Frank? The kids already ate. So did I."

"Trouble with the truck," Franklin said. He already had the telephone in his hand, dialing and trying to listen to Julie at the same time. He finished dialing and combed his fingers through his hair. He held them under his nose. He could smell the forklift exhaust clinging to the hair oil. "Suzy's at the Kwik Shop?" He was tired, and he had to force himself to picture that, to make it mean something concrete—his dog at the convenience store. "An hour ago? I drove right past there too, but the truck was giving me fits again. It just now died in the driveway." He didn't need this tonight.

"Didn't we just pay all that money for the carburetor or something?" Julie asked. "Wasn't that just last month?"

"Tom," Franklin said into the phone, "can you work tonight?"

Julie put one hand on Franklin's arm. "What about Suzy?"

"Hang on, Tom." He covered the mouthpiece. "It's work, Julie. I'll look for the dog when I get home." He removed his hand from the phone. "Tom, it's a simple job. Yank the toilet and put a new seal in. Herb set it up with his tenants. They're expecting us."

Julie turned away and stood at the sink where the dinner dishes were stacked to the rim. Franklin watched her run the water over them for a second, then turn it off again. On the other end of the phone line, Franklin's friend Tom was saying something about wanting to stay home and "chill." That was Tom all over. In Franklin's opinion, Tom had no ambition—though Franklin would never say that to Tom.

"Come on, Tom. Herb swears this one is straightforward. In and out. Not like the last time. OK, the last *times.*"

While Franklin talked Tom into working the side job, Julie stared out the kitchen window as if she expected the dog to walk back into the yard on its own. Franklin shook his head. Other people's dogs came home, not his. Why did it run away like that? It was getting hard not to personalize it.

"Thanks, Tom. I knew I could count on you," he said into the phone. "One more thing, though. Can we use your truck again?"

He hung up and went to the stove and looked in the oven window at the food Julie had warming for him. He thought he must surely be hungry, but he didn't make a move to open the oven door. When he straightened up, she was watching him.

"A couple of hours," he said. "You and the kids can look for her around here while I'm gone."

Julie stared at him.

"Where are the kids?" he said. "Did they run away too?"

———

The toilet repair job was in an old section of town Franklin rarely had reason to enter. Like most of the others on the street, the house was a two-story wreck, though he could tell that the neighborhood had been nice once. The finish carpentry on the rotting porch was intricate; the windows and doors were trimmed in moldings no one could afford anymore. But everything needed painting, and the porch floor sagged under the weight of Franklin and Tom and the plastic bucket of tools Tom carried.

Tom studied the deteriorating porch. "You'd think Herb would do something more than the minimum. How would you like to have a landlord like that guy? I mean, what would it take to paint at least?" He pulled his crinkly black hair back off his shoulders and twisted it into a ponytail and secured it with an elastic band he kept on his wrist. Franklin could remember making that same move himself, not all that long ago. Tom said, "Herb's not balanced."

"Maybe we could give him an estimate," Franklin said, seeing an opportunity for more work, because that was his whole world now, finding work and doing it. "You know, to paint." He pressed the doorbell and looked up at the yellowed varnish on the wood plank ceiling. "How difficult is painting? We could paint."

Tom shook his head sadly. "These people are getting as much out of Herb as they're going to. I tell you, the man's running on negative energy. That's why these jobs are always so bad. That's why they're always the same."

Franklin eyed Tom carefully. The "negative energy" stuff, the "Herb's not balanced." He hoped Tom wasn't going guru on him again.

He pressed the doorbell once more, with no result. Finally he pounded on the door, and a deep and ferocious barking exploded on the other side as the door reverberated with the shock of a heavy body slamming against it. The animal seemed to have been lying there in wait. Franklin could hear toenails scrabbling against wood. He and Tom both took a step back. Tom pulled a pipe wrench out of the tool bucket and held it against his leg.

There was more commotion on the other side of the door, thunderous barking, scratching. Then a woman's voice shouted over the dog's roaring, "Just a minute please. GET DOWN, MULLY! GET! GET NOW!"

"OK," Tom said. "You were right, man. This is not like the last job."

The big dog hit the inside of the door again so hard that a piece of the exterior frame sprang loose and clattered onto the porch at their feet. The woman screamed, "BLESS YOU, MULLY! SIT, BLESS YOU! SIT!"

"I'll give you that, Frank. So far, this one is a little different."

They heard the dog being dragged off into the house somewhere, and in a minute the door opened. A very old woman ushered them into a small and overheated hallway reeking of some vegetable. Cabbage, Franklin guessed. There was another smell too, but he didn't want to think about that.

The woman must have been eighty or ninety—she looked a hundred and fifty. She was wide and short and wore a pilly old wool sweater with wadded tissues jutting from the pockets and a heavy pleated skirt, in spite of the heat in the house. She was bent over, holding the collars of two identical white-muzzled Pomeranians that hopped straight up and down an inch or so off the floor next to her feet. They snapped repeatedly but produced no sound other than the faint clicking of their pointy teeth. Whatever had been doing the serious barking was nowhere in sight.

Franklin looked over the old woman's bent back into the living room. It seemed the dogs had run through it at will. A floor lamp listed against a scratched desk, its shade caved in. The remains of a woman's slipper lay among piles of chewed and shredded newspaper strewn across the floor. The carpet was covered with stains overflowing into older stains, and there were areas where the animals had dug and scratched right down through the jute backing to the old oak floor beneath it. Against one wall there was a large wing-backed sofa with an aura of dog hair clinging to it. Above it were religious pictures—weird, old-fashioned Catholic things Franklin hadn't seen the likes of since he'd dated Vicki Rotella in high school: Jesus holding his bleeding heart out in the palm of his hand, Mary floating to heaven on a little pink cloud. He noticed that the corner of one of the picture frames had been gnawed off. He'd get religion too if he had to live like this, he thought.

"Katherine O'Sullivan," the old woman said. "Herb sent you then?" She smiled warmly, squinting up at them through thick, wire-rimmed glasses as she crouched over the snapping Pomeranians. Franklin tried not to stare at the top of her head, pink and nearly hairless, or at the hump that pitched her one shoulder slightly lower than the other. "Nell's gone to lock up Mully," Katherine O'Sullivan said. "He's not so good with strangers." She turned and started down the hall, still hunched over, holding on to the little dogs. "This way, lads," she said. The dogs twisted back over their shoulders and continued their silent snapping.

Tom tapped Franklin on the shoulder. Franklin turned to find him examining the claw marks on the inside of the front door. It looked like someone had gone at it with a router. Tom whispered, "Frank, a couple more visitors, and that big fucker will be through it. We better get this job right the first time."

They followed Katherine. Halfway down the hall, a door opened narrowly and another ancient woman backed out. She pulled the door closed behind her. Franklin thought he caught a glimpse of something big pushing at the edge of it. The Pomeranians stopped their snapping. They sniffed the carpet along the threshold of the door. One of them whined softly.

"This would be Nell," Katherine said, indicating the other woman.

Nell was a thinner, taller, and straighter version of Katherine. It was clear they were sisters. She had bright green eyes that gave Franklin the impression that she had been very pretty once, although she held one hand across her nose, masking the middle portion of her face. Nell leaned and turned one ear to her sister Katherine's lips. Katherine shouted into it: "They're for the toilet!"

Yes, Franklin thought. He felt exhaustion washing over him. That's about right. For the toilet.

Nell said hello from behind her hand. Her gaze drifted off down the hall as though she preferred not to make eye contact.

"Nell's hiding," Katherine said in a whisper that her sister obviously could not hear. "It's the shingles."

"Aw, man!" Tom said. "I *knew* this was going to happen. Nobody said anything about shingles!"

The word filled the little hallway, and Nell's face colored behind her hand.

Franklin got the feeling he did not want to have this explained. How much did you really need to know about someone whose toilet you were handling? He nodded and smiled at the two women and hoped Tom wouldn't press it.

"Shingles," Tom said again. He was looking up at the ceiling of the hallway. "Frank, are they talking about the roof now? I didn't bring the extension ladder."

"Skip it, Tom."

Franklin started past the two old women to get to the bathroom door but felt a tug at one ankle and looked down to see one of the mute Pomeranians clamped to the cuff of his jeans. The dog had its front legs locked like a mule, apparently planning to drag him down the hall.

Franklin stood looking at the dog attached to his ankle. He felt the sweat building under his arms, wetting his shirt again where it had been wet and then dry several times that day. He had unloaded half a van of paint that afternoon *by hand*, because it hadn't arrived on pallets. Three hundred cases. Four gallons in each. Over twelve thousand pounds. Six tons! His neck ached. His knee throbbed where he had smashed it with a five-gallon bucket of drywall mud. He wanted to be home again in his own bathroom, lying in the tub with a beer or maybe a joint. Maybe both. And when he got home, he still had to work on the truck. And he still had to look for Suzy—the disloyal little bastard. He yanked his cuff from the Pomeranian's teeth and went into the old women's bathroom.

Tom followed him into the tiny bathroom, still scrutinizing the ceiling. "So, what's this about shingles? I mean, if we don't have the right tools. . . ."

"Tom," he said. "Please."

"Well, I don't know, man. Herb needs to get focused."

"Can we just do this?"

As Franklin and Tom crouched around the toilet, Katherine and Nell hovered in the doorway, watching. Although Katherine had released the two Pomeranians—which had stopped snapping at last and now milled around the women's ankles, sniffing and licking at the carpet—she remained stooped over nearly as far as before, and it occurred to Franklin that she couldn't stand any straighter than that.

While Tom cut the old rusted floor bolts with a hacksaw, Franklin watched one of the Pomeranians squat between the two women. The dog straightened and walked off. On the threadbare carpet next to Nell's sturdy black shoe were three dry little logs.

Tom had the bolts cut, the water supply disconnected. Now came the part Franklin hated most—lifting the toilet off. His imagination always ran a little wild at this moment. He looked away.

He wondered how much longer he would have to do these jobs. Was there a cutoff date? A specific day that came when you no longer needed the extra money, which had actually long since stopped being extra. When would that day come for him? He was twenty-four. He'd heard his father's stories about working nights at Sears while going to college when Franklin was a baby. But his father always described the night jobs as temporary, something on the way to something better. Franklin was not in college. Not anymore.

The toilet came off easily enough, revealing nothing worse than the usual hairs and water stains. They set it in the women's old cast-iron bathtub. Franklin thought things were going all right for the moment. But the seal on the toilet had been leaking for a long time, and the subflooring was shot. The sewer pipe flange floated freely in the rotted opening.

"Going to need plywood," Tom said. He wiggled the pipe flange. "Actually, this floor joist is probably a goner too." He stood and put his weight on the floor next to the hole. Franklin felt the whole room move. He glanced at the old women, but they stared at him, unaware of what it all meant.

"Christ," he muttered. "This is Herb's problem. He said a new wax ring, Tom. That's all he said. It's almost seven o'clock now."

Tom said, "What's the big deal? We're already here. I'll go pick up some three-quarter-inch ply and a two-by-ten. You stay and cut out the bad stuff."

"We're not doing it, Tom."

Tom stared at him. Franklin tried to look confident about his position. They'd been doing these side jobs together for Herb for more than a year now, and Tom had always let Franklin call the shots, and Franklin had found the responsibility satisfying in a way the warehouse job would never be. It had been fun at times, too. They even made a joke about it. At parties, with a few drinks in them, they'd call themselves Toilet Man and Bowl Boy. They'd make up ridiculous adventures for the superheroes. "No job too shitty!" was their motto. Everyone would laugh.

Tom was watching Franklin's face.

"What, Frank? We're not fixing the floor?"

"I'm beat, Tom. We'll put the new wax ring in and that's it. I have to get some sleep."

Tom looked at the sewer opening, thought about it, then turned away from Franklin. He said to the old women, "Do you ladies have another bathroom you could use for a couple of days? Upstairs, maybe?"

"Upstairs isn't ours," Katherine said. She lowered her voice and pointed toward the ceiling with one thumb. "Coloreds," she said.

"That Herb, what a peach," Tom said. "No way this building makes code for two families. What are they cooking on up there? A Coleman stove? This place burns, Herb's going away. How much money does that guy need?"

Franklin shrugged. He was amazed that Herb would pull a shot like that, though he knew for a fact that Herb was way overextended and probably sinking like everyone else. He tried to think of one person he knew who was really doing well, or even moving up at all.

He was still working on that when Tom whispered, "We going to half-ass it then?"

Franklin looked at the old women. Nell, the tall, thin one, still had one hand covering her nose. The other hand was hanging at her side, cupped against her leg. In it were the Pomeranian droppings.

He crouched over the toilet hole and tapped the floor with the end of a wrench. He kept his head down and kept tapping the floor as he spoke quietly to Tom. "I've been going since six this morning. I still have a truck to fix and a dog to find tonight."

"These ladies have a nice dog they might let you have," Tom said. He grinned. "A big-un."

"I'm serious, Tom. How soon before this wood gives out?" He tapped the floor again. "Before one of them ends up in the basement with the toilet?"

"Frank, I was just saying we could do it right if we wanted to. The truth is, they're really old. The floor will last longer than they will. I mean, if that's the way you want to handle it. It's your call."

Franklin kept tapping the floor as if testing it. What right did Tom have to make him feel so small? This was all gravy for Tom. Beer money. Weed money. He would happily stay all night, remodel the whole fucking bathroom. Franklin wanted to shout, You have no idea! You're not married! You don't have kids!

It sounded ridiculous even as he thought of it.

Finally Tom slipped the new wax ring out of its box and set it over the pipe opening. He put two new bolts upright in the flange. They looked so shiny and new against the rusted pipe, the mildewed plywood floor, the whole decrepit room. Franklin almost couldn't stand it.

They stood and went to the bathtub, lifted the toilet out, and lowered it onto the new wax ring. As Tom tightened the bolts and reattached the water supply, Franklin washed his hands at the sink, studying the rust stain that snaked from the leaking tap to the drain. How long had that drip run? Years, probably. Who cared? Who?

When Tom had the nuts down tight, he cautiously shook the toilet. Franklin saw it wobble on the rotted floor. The old women didn't seem to notice. Tom didn't look at Franklin again as he picked up his tools and wiped them off.

"Will it work?" Katherine O'Sullivan asked.

Tom flushed the toilet and watched it refill.

"It works," Franklin said to the women. "It's fine now."

"It works!" Katherine shouted into Nell's face, and they both smiled broadly.

Franklin and Tom followed the women back down the narrow hall toward the front of the house. As they passed the door to the room that held the animal called Mully, Nell dropped the hand covering her face and reached out for the doorknob. Franklin felt his heart surge. For a terrible instant he got the crazy idea that she was going to let the monster loose on them. He looked at her profile and saw that the tip of her nose was missing and that her cheeks looked gouged and red, as though they had been grated on or clawed at. When she touched the doorknob, the big dog let out a roar that started the Pomeranians silently tearing up and down the hall around their ankles. Tom dropped the tool bucket with a clamor, and Nell spun around to find Franklin looking at her. She covered her ravaged face again and scuttled past her sister as she fled into the kitchen.

"Mother of God," Katherine said, and led Franklin and Tom to the door. As she ushered them out, she said, "Bless you boys. Bless you both."

Outside on the porch, Tom said, "That's it, man. I don't think I'm up for anymore of these."

It was dark, the old street empty. Crickets chirped in the bushes along the old wooden porch. Tom pulled a joint out of his shirt pocket and lit it.

"OK," Franklin said, as Tom passed him the joint. He waited for the lecture, some New Age, simplify-your-life, get-in-touch-with-something horse shit. But Tom just said, "I mean, if you can't even laugh, what's the point?" He walked down to the van and put the tools in.

On the drive home they barely spoke. Franklin wondered if he could do the jobs alone. Lifting a toilet off and back on again alone was awkward. His back wasn't the greatest either. Still, there'd be more money—if his truck would only hold up a little longer.

They were passing the Carbide plant on Pine Avenue when Franklin looked up to see a small body of some sort lying beside the curb under one of the big halogen security lights. As they approached it, he sat up and stared at the thing, all crumpled and folded over on itself, and realized he had forgotten about Suzy the dog. Tom made no move to slow down, and Franklin almost said something. But as they passed it, he could see that the body was just some kind of scrap material, a canvas tarp or a sandbag perhaps. He couldn't tell if his heart was racing from relief or disappointment.

When they got to Franklin's house, Tom pulled into the driveway behind Franklin's truck, turned off the engine of his van, and leaned forward over the steering wheel. He rested his chin on his knuckles. "Need a hand with your rig?"

"No," Franklin said. "Thanks. I'm too tired. I'll call in late in the morning, fix it then." He started to get out.

"Nothing personal," Tom said. "Nothing against you or anything, understand? But that floor wasn't right, Frank. Those old ladies? Did you see how poor they are?"

"What are you saying, Tom?"

"I'm saying, just because they don't know any better, doesn't mean they don't deserve any better. I mean, everybody's somebody, man. You know?"

"Everybody's somebody?" Franklin said. He wondered if Tom had spent the whole drive thinking that one up. He looked at the crystal hanging from Tom's rearview mirror. He thought of the dream-catcher hoop Tom kept over his bed. He wished he could put his faith in such things. What *did* he put his faith in? Work? Certainly work. Was that any less foolish?

"Thanks for the help, Tom," he said. He closed the door and leaned in the open window. "I'll get the cash from Herb tomorrow."

Tom just shook his head and backed away.

Franklin expected a commotion when he came through the door. He expected wailing and crying about the missing dog, and he prepared himself for it. He was ready to let them know how hard, how long he had worked that day. He was ready to let them have it with both barrels.

But the house was quiet. He found Julie and the kids in the living room watching TV in the dark. Julie was on the couch, his son and daughter on the floor with their pillows and blankets. There was a bowl of pretzels on the coffee table, a can of soda and two small plastic glasses. No one heard him enter, so he stood in the entrance to the living room and watched the show they were watching. Something about priests who were also detectives, or something. It seemed an odd thing for a three-year-old and a five-year-old, but who knew what they did when he wasn't there. The light from the TV flickered over his family. Their faces looked like they were made of plaster.

He made a move to turn away, and his daughter saw his form in the shadows. She screamed and scrabbled backwards across the carpet on her bottom, legs flailing. His son bolted from the floor like a rabbit and ran and buried his face in Julie's lap. Julie gasped.

"Jesus, Frank! You scared us half to death." She patted the boy's head. She held her other hand against her collarbone. "Standing there like a spook. Good God."

His daughter recovered first. "You scared us, Daddy," she said. Then she laughed. "Daddy, Suzy came back. She came home!"

His wife said, "It's true. She just walked right back into the yard and sat down. She'd been in the river, was covered with mud. I locked her in the garage. It was the funniest thing, honey. We were just going out to look for her, and there she was, out front. Can you believe it?"

They were all looking at him then, his daughter still on the floor, his wife and son on the couch. Franklin wondered what they wanted now.

"Can you believe it? Can you believe it?" the boy said, parroting his mother. He started marching around the coffee table. "Suzy! Suzy! Suzy! Believe it!" he shouted. "Believe it!"

It makes no difference, Franklin thought. The dog would get out again tomorrow, or the next day, or next week, and he wouldn't have the hundred dollars then either. Or if he did, he sure wouldn't have the hundred and fifty the next time she escaped, or whatever they'd want the time after that.

Sooner or later it would come down to him making the decision to leave her there rotting at the pound. It would seem like a game to her at first—for three or four days, she'd lie in her cage, waiting for him. But a stranger would come instead, and he would inject her, or gas her, or decompress her until her lungs collapsed, or whatever they did to destroy animals these days.

Franklin wondered what they would do with the body. Cremation, he supposed. It made him think about his animal cemetery. Every kid must have done that at one time, he thought. His was behind the garage. His mother had tried to plant vegetables there, but there was not enough sunlight. The earth was soft, and the first thing he had buried was a robin that had struck the living room window and fell stunned into his mother's tiger lilies. Though it regained consciousness, and Franklin had kept it in a shoe box and tried to feed it, the bird died by the end of the day. There was a lesson in that, but he missed it; he could see that now. He buried the robin deep, marked the grave with a popsicle-stick cross, and sprinkled "holy water" over it from a ketchup bottle. For the rest of that summer, there seemed to be dead animals everywhere he looked. He could hardly bury them as fast as he found them. Mice, frogs, turtles, even a bat once—flattened by cars. Baby birds fallen from nests. A squirrel dead below the power lines with a tiny burn hole on one leg. Franklin had buried and blessed them all. That was the summer of dead animals. That was a long time ago.

"Oh," Julie said. "I almost forgot. Herb just called a minute before you got home. He's a funny guy. He makes me laugh. He's got another job for you. I can't remember it all."

Something on TV caught her eye. She leaned forward, picking up the soda can and sipping from it without taking her eyes off the set.

Franklin was really tired now. He felt his bad knee buckle slightly and slumped into the wall, pressed his face against the textured plaster.

Herb had another job. It didn't matter what it was. Franklin would take it. He would take what Herb offered. Who didn't know that? Herb knew it. Julie knew it. And Franklin knew it, too. He would do what he had to do. Leave the dog unclaimed at the pound? You bet. He was sure of that now. If it came right down to it, he might do anything. He might leave them all there.

"Anyway," Julie said, turning away from the TV. "I just remembered what Herb wanted. . . ."

But Franklin was listening to something else now, a sound coming from the garage on the other side of the wall. Something scratching. It was the dog. Suzy. She was digging at something, working at it with her nails—the garage door, the wall, something. For the longest time, he stood there listening to her scratching. Scratching to get out.

He found himself looking up at the wall he was leaning against. There was a settlement crack running along the corner where it met the ceiling. There was a row of small bulges in the plaster where the drywall nails had popped. There was a stain in the ceiling about a foot out from the wall, a water stain, brown and shaped something like Texas, and it meant the roof had leaked. He was amazed that he had never noticed it before. None of it. Who knew how many more things there were to be repaired, right there in his own home, if he just looked close enough to see them?

Franklin heard Julie talking again. But he was busy, already planning what it was going to take to fix things.

Those Little
Foreign Beauties

This was the plan. We'd agree to buy about four hundred pounds of frozen food—vegetables, meat, a number of things coated with bread crumbs and already fried. The company would finance a huge freezer for us to keep it all in.

I'm not educated, but I think I have what they call native intelligence, and it didn't sound bad to me. Sheila was not so sure. She was giving the salesman a hard time.

"That's a bunch of food," she said. "A bunch."

"How many times have you had unexpected company and nothing to offer?" the guy asked. He avoided Sheila's glare, aiming the question at me across our kitchen table.

"How many payments?" Sheila wanted to know.

"Twenty-four." Again to me. "Two years without shopping cares. The crowds. The lines. You think the rich wait in lines?" He shook his head as if the idea made him dizzy. He rolled his eyes my way, like he and I knew something my wife would never figure out.

Sheila opened her mouth to say something, but the phone rang.

I grabbed it off the wall behind me. It was Smitty next door. He'd seen the Food Systems sign on the salesman's car and couldn't resist. I'm surprised he didn't just come right over.

"Are you receptive to some friendly advice?" Smitty said. Not even a hello. "Weekly shopping. All the studies show it to be the most economical approach."

That was pure Smitty. Dr. Bernard Smith, P, H, and D, anthropologist, and what I'd have to call a classy guy. There in the neighborhood, he wanted to be known as Smitty. I had tried Doctor Smith, Bernard, even Bernie, but he insisted. I'll give him credit, he tried to fit in—drove a pickup, popped a few tops with me after work from time to time. Still, there was something superior about him, and it showed up every time he opened his mouth.

At the moment, he was rattling off statistics on purchasing power and food prices. I held the phone to my ear and smiled at the salesman, at Sheila. They looked like they were about to start clawing each other's eyes.

"Smitty, I have to go."

"Just let me add this caveat—"

"No, really," I said. I hung up and sat back down.

Caveat! God, I wished I could spout off shit like that.

The salesman cranked up his smile again and shut Sheila out of the picture. "Take it from me," he said. "It's the way the bright boys do things." He pressed one finger against the contract and pushed it my way across the tabletop. "You think Iacocca runs out to the store every two days?"

Sheila looked at her nails.

I reached for the pen.

Plans. I go for all of them. I figure it's the only way a working guy can get ahead and improve himself in this world. Leave nothing to chance. And it's nice to feel like you belong, like you're part of something too. I sign up for book clubs, record and tape deals, every kind of insurance plan imaginable. Now I own books I can't read, music I can't stomach, and insurance I can't afford.

Before the frozen food deal, it was a vocabulary growth program: Word Muscle. The ad said, "You're not stupid. Why talk that way?" All I could think of was Smitty and the words he used, how those little foreign beauties made Sheila sigh out loud and left me wondering if I'd ever catch up. Had to have it.

Word Muscle came with a thirty-pound dictionary, a thesaurus, and software I still haven't figured out. One more plan gone bad.

Sheila can usually joke about these little setbacks ("I like a man with a big dictionary!"), but this food thing turned out worse than usual.

A week after we signed the contract, I was on the job site when Sheila called. Food Systems had delivered the groceries, but there was no freezer on the truck. Sheila was going ape.

I hung up and said to my boss, "Carl, I have to take the afternoon. I got half a ton of frozen shit melting in my garage."

Carl was right out of the classroom—wore his hard hat like a crown, and made it clear that he was never going to have to strap on a tool belt and roll around in the dirt with the rest of us. Got a big kick out of my Word Muscle period.

"Frozen shit, huh? Cooking lessons now?"

I know there must be a word, the perfect word, that would have caught him like four fingers to the windpipe, a word that would have knocked that bachelor-of-science grin all the way back to his molars. All I could come up with was "dickhead," and I was out the door.

When I got home, Sheila was sitting in the kitchen in her swimsuit, eating ice cream out of the box, determined not to lose it all and obviously pissed. Outside, the temperature was pushing ninety, winds whipping the dust through the dead brown grass I got with my Lifetime Lawn plan. Sheila had put as much of the frozen food as she could into the little freezer above our fridge. More of it was crammed in the fridge itself, the setting turned up to its coldest.

I watched her spoon some ice cream into her mouth. She licked the spoon, top and bottom. It made me hungry and more than a little horny, but she gave me a look hard enough to scratch glass.

"Where's the rest?" I asked.

She stood and pulled open the back door.

There were stacks of frozen boxes sweating in the stuffy heat of the garage. Broccoli, corn, carrots, and peas. Breaded scallops, breaded fish fillets, breaded shrimp. White paper bundles of meat already starting to sag under their own weight. A thin puddle was spreading through the garage floor dust.

"How does this happen to us?" Sheila said. "I'd like to know that. Can somebody tell me that?"

I hoped she didn't really want an answer for that. That would have been a little out of my range for sure. I would have liked to just write it all off as one more disaster. We could go out for a couple of margaritas, forget the whole pile until Monday, and then call those bastards and tell them where to park it. But Sheila was taking it hard. She stood in front of the food pile in her bathing suit with the ice cream box in her hand, the ice cream gone to liquid and running down her leg.

"We're not paying for this!" she said. She whipped her spoon into the corner. It fell behind the lawn mower.

I was beginning to wonder how many times we'd have to go through this sort of thing, how many failures it would take before things started working out. I thought maybe I should throw something too. Then I saw that a different approach was needed.

I went out to my truck, hoping to avoid Smitty next door, not in any mood for a dose of his advice at this time. His front door swung open with a bang before I got halfway down my driveway. It was Smitty's wife, Joann, stepping out onto the porch carrying a small suitcase. She'd been crying, and if I didn't know better, I'd have said there was a bruise under her left eye. That came as a bit of a shock to me. I mean, Smitty and Joann slugging it out? No way. I said hi, and she just nodded my way and dabbed at the corner of her eye with a hanky. She was still holding the suitcase but didn't make a move toward their car.

I wondered if I should say something about her eye. I really didn't know Joann, a nice-looking woman in her forties with the thin body and thick helmet of hair that all women married to guys like Smitty seemed to have. Even though they had lived next door for two years, it had always been plain to me that Smitty and Joann were different, better somehow. I used to wonder why they didn't find a nicer neighborhood. At first I thought maybe he was studying the working class—you know, move-in-and-live-with-the-natives stuff. But it turned out to be a matter of money—just like everybody else. "I've got some plans," he told me one time. "My book is starting to sell." (His book is called *Language, Man, and Meaning: Beyond Numb Chumpsky*, or something. I tried to read it. What a snoozer.) He said, "Another year or two. The kids are almost finished with school. With Joann part time at the college, I can make my move. Not that this isn't a perfectly nice place to live, vis-à-vis the current economy."

Veez-a-vee! Jesus, but he could come up with them. I could only guess what he'd have to say about the meltdown in my garage.

Joann held the hanky to her face and sobbed.

"You OK?" I asked. I took a step toward her.

She shooed me away with the hanky, looking out over my head up the street. It was clear she was waiting for someone.

The driveway was like an oven in the afternoon sun, the blacktop so soft you could dig it out with your fingernail. I thought of all the food baking in my garage. Joann seemed pretty sad, and I'm not heartless, but what can you really do for somebody you have to look up to? I slid into my truck and headed for the store.

Ice. We needed ice. They had nothing but cubes at the Kwik Shop; I took every bag in the place. Carnival Liquors had blocks, a dozen; I cleaned them out, too. I hit the Bottle Barn and Moreli's Family Market and headed back home with ice piled to the top of my tailgate. It was going to be a bad weekend for picnickers in this town.

When I got back, Joann was gone from their porch. Still no sign of Smitty. So far, so good. I unloaded the ice into my garage and shut the door again.

It looked like an igloo. Blocks and bags of ice stacked four feet high and nearly as wide each way surrounded the food pile. The runoff ran out under the door like a little creek.

Sheila was calmer. She was also halfway through a gin and tonic big enough to drown in. Like I said, she was calmer. She just stared at the ice pile and said, "I'll fix you one of these."

Now we were getting somewhere. I pictured a quiet evening at home, two or three more G&Ts, and a certain bikini kicked into the corner of the bedroom. But when Sheila finally came back out to the garage with my drink, Smitty was with her. He was wearing Bermuda shorts and a T-shirt with cartoon cavemen on it. On his feet were high-top Reeboks unlaced, the way kids were wearing them—a combination of attempted hipness and the extreme dorkiness that pretty much summed him up. He walked out of the kitchen and into the garage behind Sheila like he lived there.

I should have known he could sniff out something like this. I braced myself for what he'd have to say, but he was quiet as we put lawn chairs in a half circle around the edge of the food like it was a campfire. Sheila stuffed two bottles of tonic water into the ice and set the lime and a paring knife on a breadboard next to the Tanqueray bottle her folks had sent us the Christmas before. The three of us held our drinks in our laps, slipped off our shoes, and sat with our bare feet in the puddle.

For a while we all just sat there, sweating and watching the pile melt. Nobody said anything. I didn't mention seeing Joann on the porch. I couldn't even guess how to approach that, or even if I should. I was more concerned right then about how small Smitty was going to make me feel in front of Sheila this time. I expected him to start any time, making me twist and squirm the way he could. A bag of cubes shifted, and some meat pies fell over onto the floor.

Smitty was still silent. I'd never seen him at a loss for words. Something was very wrong. There were no "caveats," "fiats," "codas," or "per ses." Nobody was "qua" anything else. And, for the first time since I'd known him, Smitty had not declared anything I was doing to be "surreal."

Suddenly, right out of the blue, he started talking about our neighbors Nancy and Bruce Halverson. They lived three houses down, on the other side of Smitty. I barely knew them.

"What do you honestly think of Nancy Halverson," he blurted out, as if we had been talking about her right along. "You think she dresses smart, right? You've seen her dolled up."

Sheila gave me a look that seemed to say, "Where in the hell did that come from?" I shrugged.

"I mean, can the woman dress or what?" Smitty said.

Sheila squirmed a little, looked down at her swimsuit. There was a pink ice cream stain on her left breast.

"No, wait," Smitty said. He put one hand on Sheila's knee. "I'm not saying that the way you think. Just listen to this. Nancy Halverson buys a new wardrobe every spring and every fall. I don't mean a few outfits. I mean a goddamn wardrobe. That's her own word for it. Wardrobe. She's got more shoes than the first lady and dresses she hasn't even cut the tags off."

He stopped, knocked back what was left in his glass. He said, "Fix me a piece of lime, would you, honey?" He still had one hand on Sheila's knee.

Smitty seemed to be cheering up a bit, telling this story. But I had this creeping feeling he was going somewhere with it that I'd regret. I kept an eye on him as he splashed a whole lot of gin in his glass and very little tonic. Sheila cut him a piece of lime and plopped it in for him. I hated the way that looked—her waiting on him like that.

"So, anyway," he said. "They're maxed out on every credit card they can get, and spring comes and goes and Nancy's still going shopping somehow, and Bruce can't figure out how she's making the money stretch. Then, a couple weeks ago, Bruce gets home early or something and gets to the mailbox before she does. There's a certified letter from the bank. His house is being foreclosed on. Nancy hasn't made a payment in five months!"

Smitty laughed. It was loud and fake and so forced that it made him choke on his drink. He held his glass high over his head and pounded on his chest with his other fist.

Sheila and I just looked at each other.

"Jesus. Are they going to lose it?" I asked.

"What?" Smitty said. He got his breath back, but he looked confused by the question. His face was red all the way to the top of his forehead.

"The house? Will Bruce and Nancy lose the house?"

"How do I know? What am I, a lawyer?"

Whatever he'd found funny about Bruce and Nancy had passed. He was moping again. "I was just trying to cheer you two up. Just being friendly," he said, with a real lost-puppy look that was making me nervous. Any second now I was expecting one of his comments, some Latin zinger that would leave me grinning and nodding like I knew what he meant, while the sweat ran down my back because I didn't have a clue.

All he said was, "You two don't know how lucky you are." It came out a whimper. "There, I've said it. Lucky." He looked like he was actually going to start crying.

Sheila said, "Smitty, you OK?"

The tenderness in her voice made me so jealous I felt my jaw locking up.

"Smitty?" Sheila said again, leaning way over now to look up into his long face. She was practically spilling out of her swimsuit, but Smitty didn't give her a glance. He just stared down into his glass.

"Yeah, I'm fine. I'm swell," he said. "But who really gives a shit?"

"Well . . . " Sheila started.

"No," Smitty said, sitting straight up in his chair suddenly, like he was getting tough now. "Just fuck it," he said. Only there were no real balls behind it. You could tell it was not a word the anthropologist had a lot of opportunity to use that way. It came out more a chirp than anything else, and I started laughing. He looked at me directly, eyes bulging.

"What? Is that word not allowed in this garage?"

That did it. I howled. Sheila cut me a look that could have refrozen the whole food pile, but I couldn't stop.

"What?" Smitty screamed. He jumped up out of his lawn chair, and it collapsed behind him. "Women fail to make house payments! They buy shoes instead! People order food they can't afford and watch it spoil! A man's wife just decides to up and screw some pissant, half-assed, grad-student poet! And I'm supposed to watch my language? Is that it?"

He was standing over the food pile, holding his glass in front of him in two hands, the muscles in his neck knotting like a weight lifter's. OK, maybe this wasn't so funny after all. Joann left him for a poet? Jesus, that was pretty awful. Still, I had to admit it was kind of a treat—seeing what happened to Smitty's vocabulary when he finally had something real to say.

But enough was enough.

I tried to serious up. Looking at Smitty's problem, at Bruce Halverson's, I should have been grateful. I knew that. But right there in front of us was plenty to remind me that my life wasn't exactly working out perfectly either.

In a minute we were all seated again around the melting food. Smitty leaned back in his chair. He closed his eyes and put his feet up on the ice bags, pressed his drink against his forehead, and slowly shook his head back and forth.

"Smitty," I said. "How about some dinner?" I gave the pile a good shove with one foot, and it slumped around his chair. "Go ahead," I said. "Pick something out. Whatever you want."

Smitty shook his head. No. He wasn't hungry. And he wasn't talking anymore either. He was all out of words for the time being. Big words. Small words. Foreign and domestic. He was out.

I knew what he needed. I'd been planning to save this one for some special occasion when I could blindside him with it. It was from my Word Muscle days. I'd seen it in italic somewhere and had looked it up. I'm convinced the ones in italic are the good ones, the ones you can do real damage with. I had only a vague idea what it meant, but I had practiced pronouncing it for weeks, sometimes saying it over and over to myself out loud in the truck as I drove to and from work. I loved the sound of it, so foreign, so impressive.

"Come on, Smitty," I said. "It's probably just one of those *fin de siècle* things."

I purposely mispronounced it. "Finn-da-sickle," I said. Like it was some kind of Scandinavian ice cream bar.

That was a gift for Smitty, and sure enough, he rose like a trout and started correcting me. But that was fine too, because Sheila was looking at me like I had grown a third eye. And it was clear to me that for the first time in a long while now, she was maybe just a teeny bit impressed.

Dealer's Choice

——————

Darlene knows she was asked to play only because they needed a fifth for the game, but she's worked seventeen straight days now, and the Friday night options for entertainment on this little island are not good. She is determined to be one of the boys. There's the cook, two maintenance electricians from the fish plant, a Filipino man she's seen driving a forklift on the dock, and her. She hasn't won a pot all night and is down almost thirty dollars, but she's promised herself she's not going to get bent out of shape over every damn thing. That was the whole point of coming all the way to this rain-soaked chunk of Alaskan rock: getting away from the pressures of city life, learning to relax. Anyway, this is only a two-dollar-limit game, and with the salmon season in full swing and the cannery running three shifts, there are plenty of dishes to wash, and she's getting all the overtime she can handle.

"What's the game, again?" Darlene asks. She pours a little more tequila in her plastic cup, another splash of Mountain Dew. The absurdly green concoction looks and tastes like radiator coolant, but it's almost impossible to get alcohol in Chignik Bay, and the pint of Cuervo was the only thing she'd been able to score under the table. She pours a bit more into the Mountain Dew. What the hell, it's a friendly game.

"I just called it. Seven Stud, Follow the Queen," the cook says. He's already dealt two cards facedown in front of everyone and is about to turn the next one up. He's mid-forties, former marines. He's told Darlene all about it—'Nam, Cambodia—but he's gone to fat now; kept the haircut, lost the muscle. He wears a short-cropped beard that extends from just under his eye sockets, down across two substantial chins, and all the way into the collar of his bulging "Spawn 'Till You Die" T-shirt. It gives Darlene the impression that his whole body is carpeted with the same half-inch, translucent, gray-white hairs. Along with the belly, the slouch, and the watery pink eyes, the effect is undeniable: Everyone calls him Possum.

Possum pauses and lets Billy, the younger of the two electricians, break a twenty and buy more of the red plastic wire connector nuts they are using for chips. The other electrician, Walter, a late-middle-aged man with the full beard and leathery wrinkles of a lifetime sourdough, is the banker for the game. While they work out the transaction, Darlene takes a swallow of her drink and tries to remember what Follow the Queen is exactly. These guys play strictly kitchen-table poker, with so many wild cards and twists on the last card and such that it's hard to keep track of them all: Low Chicago, High Chicago, Roll Your Own, Crisscross, Royal Birth—it goes on and on.

They are playing in Possum's room, one of the elementary classrooms at the village school, rented out during the summer months to cannery workers. There are chalkboards and bulletin boards and tiny wood and metal desks stacked almost to the ceiling in one corner. The table they are playing on tonight barely clears Darlene's knees, and she can't help feeling they should be working with white paste and construction paper instead of a poker deck.

While Billy counts out his new wire nuts, she stands and stretches her legs, pulls the tail of her blouse out of her jeans, and smoothes it over her hips with her palms. Leaning into the kitchen dish sink all day has put a knot in her neck that a sailor would be proud of, and now she throws her head back and rolls it from side to side. When she looks back down at the game, she realizes that Billy has finished counting his chips and they are all staring up at her from their tiny molded plastic chairs.

"Follow the Queen?" she says, easing back into her chair. She raises her eyebrows quizzically. "Tell me again how it goes."

Possum clutches the deck tighter and pouts, letting Darlene know that he doesn't plan to repeat himself. The truth is, when he explained the game, she was chatting, doing some innocent flirting with young Billy. She casts a needy eye his way again now.

"Remember, we played it earlier?" Billy says, smiling. He's smitten for sure, and he's a real cutie too. But he is way too young for her, and in any case, the other thing she promised herself when she signed on for the summer was that she would do the whole stretch without any of that kind of action for once in her life. Those were her two resolutions: For the next three months she was not going to get angry and she was not going to get laid. She had a vague theory that if she could avoid one of those she might avoid the other.

"Follow the Queen," Billy prompts her again. "You know."

"I think so," Darlene says.

"Follow the bitch," Possum says. "Follow the mop-squeezing bitch." He shoots Darlene an exaggerated, fake-apologetic glance, like he's suddenly realized there is a lady present in the room. He makes it look playful, but when he dealt this game earlier, he said the same rude thing, and there is a trace of heat in his words that Darlene recognizes right off.

It's just talk, she tells herself. Marine stuff. Construction guy talk. She's heard way worse every day of her life—who hasn't? She is not going to let it bother her.

"What's wild?"

Possum ignores her and begins flipping the cards, announcing each one out loud, as though no one else at the table can read them. "Billy gets a six. A nine of hearts for Walter. Roberto gets—"

"Are queens wild?" She's doing it now half to piss him off. "Are they? Queens?"

Possum closes his eyes and peels the next card off the top of the deck. He holds it there upright in front of him but doesn't look at it. Through clenched jaws he says, "If a queen turns up, the next card, the one that follows, becomes the wild card. Comprendo?"

"Why, thank you," she says. "Thank you, Possum."

When he opens his eyes, his face collapses. "Well, wouldn't you just fucking know it?" He throws the card, the queen of clubs, to the man sitting on Darlene's right, the Filipino named Roberto. Roberto is a good player, quiet and smart, and he takes every bet seriously. At times, she gets the impression he pretends not to speak English well in order to avoid all the table talk. She's seen plenty of real players like Roberto, back in Las Vegas.

"Now, you will be getting de wile card," Roberto says to her as the queen settles in front of him. His accent thickens even more, as though he almost forgot to use it. "Next card. See? Pallow de queen."

"Natch," Possum says. "She *would* get the candy." He turns another card and flips it to her. "Seven. Sevens are wild. For now, anyway. If another queen rolls, everything changes." He deals himself an ace of diamonds. "It's your bet," he says to her. "With the seven wild, you got a pair, at the very least. You *do* understand that?"

She peeks at her two down cards, although she just looked at them as they were dealt to her—the move of a rookie, she's aware, because serious stud players, like Roberto, for instance, always wait until they get their first faceup card before looking in the hole. Who knows why? Maybe it's some kind of macho self-discipline thing, a puny self-inflicted challenge in the absence of real hardships like wars and such. It reminds her a bit of her first husband, Greg, and his "one match" campfires. You'd think he gained penis length or something.

"Yoo hoo," Possum says. "Anybody in there?"

"Wait," she says. "I have to think."

"Don't threaten us." He gets a smile all around.

She takes her time staring at the pair of sevens she has in the hole to match the one faceup. Three wild cards. It sets her heart pounding way out of proportion to the low limit in this game. She feels heat rising to her face and tugs at the neck of her blouse.

"Two dollars," she says, throwing out eight wire nuts. "That's the most I can bet, right?" She pulls the pin from her hair and shakes it out so that it falls, blond and shimmering, over her shoulders and down the front of her blouse. "This is fun!"

"Give a woman a wild card . . . " Possum says. He rolls his eyeballs skyward, but Darlene notices they come back to linger at the point where her hair ends along the ridge of her breasts. She fingers a button as though she might unfasten it. He toys with the pile of wire nuts in front of him. "Oh, how I'd love to raise," he says. "There is *nothing* in this world I would like better than that. Nothing."

Darlene can think of one or two things he'd like better. She says, "I hope I'm not stopping you."

"I'm not even going to try to explain." He simply matches her bet. Billy and Walter both see the bet too, though there was no question that they would. They truly seem to be playing for fun, and Darlene believes it's because they probably make the unbelievable wages everyone says they do.

The Filipino, Roberto, cuts his dark eyes at her, then back to his hand, carefully considering his queen and whatever he's got in the hole, then back to her again. She raises her drink and salutes him. He slides his two dollars' worth of wire nuts in. "I don't know 'bout dis one." He motions toward Darlene with his head.

She holds the cup to her lips and barely touches the liquid with the tip of her tongue. Across the table, young Billy's neck goes red. Possum glares at her.

"Pot's right," he says. Still looking at her, he takes a sip of his beer, dries his fingers on his T-shirt, and starts dealing the next round. "Follow the ball-buster. A jack for Billy. Nine of spades for Walter makes a pair. A jack for Roberto. And a queen for Missy! Free ride's over now, little lady. Sevens are no longer wild, and the next card is mine."

He's puffing up like the big sculpins and Irish lords she catches on a hand line off the cannery pier after work those nights when there's even less than nothing to do on the island. His eyes bulge as though he's come up from a great depth. He's sprouting pectoral fins, gill plates.

"And the new wild card is . . . " He drags this out good. Holding the deck up to eye level in his left palm, he slides the top card halfway off, peeks under it, and flips it faceup on the table in front of himself. "A deuce! Deuces are the new wild card." He pushes a pile of wire nuts into the pot. "Pair of aces bets two." Everyone sees the bet, and Possum reins in his excitement enough to start dealing the next round.

Just to fry him, Darlene is about to turn the charm on Billy again when the door to the room opens and in walks a dark young girl in a Bering Pride Seafoods windbreaker and hot-pink Lycra tights. She's about fifteen or so, obviously Aleut and something else too. The name George is stitched into the too-large nylon jacket in flowery cursive. The girl says to Roberto, "Dad, can I sleep at Mom's house tonight?"

"OK, I don't care," Roberto says. "Long as she's not drinking."

"She doesn't have anything," the girl says. "Nobody does." She looks hungrily at the beer cans in front of Possum and the electricians, at the bottle of Cuervo next to Darlene's Mountain Dew. She turns to leave.

"And that guy's not there either?" Roberto says to her. "Right?" He glances around the table uncomfortably. Billy and Walter make a show of studying their cards, but Possum is staring openly at the girl as though searching for some mark on her, something that will describe her role in whatever little drama her father is hinting at. Darlene has not been on the island long enough to know the particulars, but Roberto's embarrassment gives her a pretty clear picture of what the story is.

"He's out on the seiner," the girl says to her father.

As Roberto considers that, Darlene looks the girl over and sees it all: the suede fringed boots caked with island mud; the look-at-me rings, two and three on a finger; the chipped Fire-and-Ice nail polish; the lavender eyeliner, way too wide, too thick, and all wrong in any case for that beautiful olive-brown skin. She can see in the girl's eyes the despair at her entrapment on this rock, the loathing for this little village. And she sees the romance of an older guy too—a guy with money, fish money, crab money, paychecks accumulating for weeks at sea.

The girl catches Darlene studying her, and she looks straight back, staring longingly at all that blond hair, at Darlene's fine, hard breasts. Darlene can see her calculating the wide swath she could cut through the village boys with equipment like that. She wants to say to her, "Oh, honey, slow down. Slow way, way down." And then the girl is gone, back out into the rainy Aleutian night.

Roberto pulls on his face. He looks a little pale. "You have children?" he asks Darlene.

"A boy, sixteen," she says, and hears herself rush to add, "I was only seventeen myself when I had him." But it's clear they are not concerned with her age. However, when she says, "He lives with his father back in Vegas," everybody comes alert at the name of the city.

Roberto's eyes narrow, wariness cresting around the rims. "You a dealer?" The others tense as though he's about to unmask a monster among them, a serial killer, a vampire, a feminist. Billy and Walter look like they are going to make a dash for the door.

"No way." She laughs, trying to defuse this. "Keno runner for a while. Mostly, though, I was a stripper."

That does it. Roberto is not interested, his mind on his daughter again. But Billy and Walter sit up a little taller in their seats, and Possum is staring at her shirt front. OK, if this is the way it's going to be.

"Started at the Palomino Club on my twenty-first birthday. That was the first totally nude club in Vegas." She emphasizes "totally." She doesn't have a clue if that's true about the club and doesn't care. "I was *so* hot." She shakes her head, as if remembering times too wild to talk about.

"You never mentioned that before," Possum says. He makes it sound as though he's been cheated somehow.

She pours on the honey. "I feel like I know you guys a little better now and I can open up a little, is all."

Roberto is too inscrutable for her to figure, but she can feel the vibrations from the other three coming across the floor under the table. The overhead light flickers, and it's not just the big cannery generators and refrigeration units either. Billy has given up pretending not to stare at her now, and she has to admit it is kind of sweet. Maybe the age difference is not such a big deal. For a moment, she seriously considers it.

Nah, not this time. But it is tempting. It's always tempting.

You'd think the cold, the constant rain on this island would put a damper on all that, yet sometimes she listens to the other women in the bunkhouse talking—they're girls really, coeds working on the slime line for the fat cannery paychecks that will give them another two semesters at schools Darlene has never even heard of. She hears them talking about guys, and it amazes her that even after twelve, fourteen back-cramping hours at a wet, steel table packing salmon roe or gutting two tons of slimy cod in a room cooled to near freezing, they still have the energy to pair up with their male counterparts. And where, exactly, *do* they go? Is there an old mattress, a scratchy wool blanket maybe, frayed and crisscrossed with pecker tracks, out there somewhere under the dripping, fog-drenched alder bushes?

"Come on, deal," Roberto says. He's turning one of the plastic wire nuts over and over in his fingers, walking it across his knuckles and back again. He's muttering to himself and shaking his head. "Women gonna be whores, you can't stop them. You can't. No way." Then he looks up suddenly and sees Darlene watching him. "Don't listen to me," he says to her. "My daughter. She's making me estupid."

"There's a lot of that going around," Possum says.

"Whorishness or stupidity?" Darlene asks him.

"Sometimes both," Possum says and deals another round, ignoring Roberto's comments and too preoccupied now to bother reading off the cards as they fall even faster than usual. Darlene can't even guess what has him more wound up, the vision of her naked, gyrating bottom or the fact that he's the only one in the kitchen crew who knows about it. "Another six for Billy makes a pair. Walter gets a five to go with his pair of nines. A king for Roberto's queen and the jack—straightening nicely. And a four for our dancing dishwasher here, no help." When he drops a second ace next to his wild deuce, everyone groans. He's apparently forgotten to swallow since hearing her revelation and spits all over himself as he says, "Three aces bets two bucks."

"Three fucking bullets," Billy moans. "I should have gone fishing tonight." But he puts his money in.

Walter shakes his head. "I am fishing." But he sees the bet too.

"I can beat three aces right now," Roberto says. He reaches for his chips. "Two dollar, and two more." He slams them down on the table hard enough to knock over Darlene's empty cup.

This stuff with his daughter, his ex-wife, whoever the guy out on the seiner is, and whatever he's been up to with the girl, it's definitely getting to Roberto. It's a hell of a thing to take advantage of, but, push comes to shove, a woman's got to look after herself, and Roberto is absolutely right in any case: There is no way to stop that young thing now. Nobody knows that any better than Darlene does. She counts out four dollars' worth of wire nuts. "I'm in."

Possum sees Roberto's raise without comment for once, as do Billy and Walter.

"Pot's right, again." Possum wipes his forehead. There is a huge mound of the red wire connectors in the middle of the table and still two cards to go—one up, one down.

Just as he's about to deal the next up card, Darlene says, "My second husband, James, picked all my music, made me practice my numbers all day till I ached in the worst places from those deep bends." She directs that at Billy, but she can just about hear the gears grinding in every brain at the table, the fluids backing up in other regions of their bodies. "James was very involved. Used to dress me up for my act and everything."

Possum throws the card so hard it flies past Billy and flutters off the table.

"Your husband?" Walter says, as Billy fumbles around on the floor for his card. He takes off his cap and looks at it. He studies the words OTIS ELEVATOR for a moment. "Your own husband dressed you to strip?"

"Oh yeah. He was always there when I performed, too, except at special private functions at the hotels. If I was slack or didn't look like I really wanted to be there, he'd mark me down. Then, when we got home, he'd punish me." It's her turn to roll her eyes, like she's a little embarrassed to be talking about such personal matters.

She mixes another tequila antifreeze while she lets them try to imagine what sort of punishments a man would have to cook up for a woman who did naked squat thrusts for a living. Roberto clears his throat and looks away from her. Billy and Walter lift their beers to their lips, sip, and then lower the cans again in such perfect unison that it looks like they've been rehearsing the move for months. Possum deals the rest of the round, sets the deck down, and reaches under the table with both hands to adjust the front of his sweatpants.

Billy is now showing two sixes, a jack, and an ace. Walter has a pair of nines with a five and the last ace in the deck. Roberto caught a ten, and thus has four to the open-ended straight on board, king high. Darlene has the queen, the four, and, to her utter amazement, two sevens showing now to match the two she has in the hole. Possum gets a six to go with his three aces, no help. He bets two bucks anyway, but with all the aces accounted for, it's clear his heart isn't in it. Still, deuces are wild, and he's got the only one showing. Billy and Walter call.

Roberto apparently has the straight and is hoping to blast anyone he can out before they catch a full house. "See your two, and raise two more," he says. He puts his last eight wire nuts and two damp dollar bills into the pot.

"God, this is fun! I feel like dancing," Darlene says. Four pairs of eyes snap up. "I really do. I wish we had some music. I could show you the moves I won the big competition with at the Flamingo. Anyway, I'll see Roberto's raise and raise again." She puts her six dollars' worth in.

Possum squirms, but Darlene knows there's no way he's going to fold three aces at this point. It's a matter of pride; it's a matter of balls. He runs his hand over the stubble field of his throat, drops it to his lap, and tugs on himself. He calls the two raises. Billy and Walter finally fold out. Darlene offers them a look of pure sympathy, as though not having cards is a very sad disease they've all struggled with at one time or another, and she wishes she could just take them in her arms and hold them to her breast to comfort them. Roberto calls her raise with a sigh, and the pot is right again.

"Here we go," Possum says. "Three players now." He deals the last cards facedown. One to Roberto, then Darlene, then himself. He looks at his card quickly, and she watches a fat smile creep across his face. "Two bucks," he says. "Roberto? You want to raise me now, ol' buddy?" He's wearing a smirk you could park a truck in.

Anyone with eyes can see he caught some power on the last card. Either he paired something up to make a full house, or he got another wild deuce and now has four aces. Darlene feels Roberto watching her on her right as he thinks about his move. She picks at the corner of the card Possum just dealt her, but she doesn't look under it. Instead, she removes her earrings, her necklace, and her watch and puts them all in a pile next to her chips.

Roberto shakes his head. "Dealer just got something good. Woman don't even need to look at her last card. What am I doing in this hand?" He turns his straight over and throws it into the middle of the table, muttering something in his dialect that it's probably just as well no one at the table can understand.

"Just you and me," Possum says. "Isn't it romantic?"

"Two bucks," she says.

"And two more back at you." Possum dumps more wire nuts on the pile before she's even finished sliding hers in. His hand brushes the top of hers over the pot. "OK, *now* tell us about your dancing," he says. "Come on, distract us. Distract me."

She looks right into his little pink eyes, and says, "I was working a private party at the Hilton one Halloween, conventioneers. I gave the bellhops a cut to set it up for me. These were computer guys of some sort, very straight looking, math teacher haircuts and white short-sleeve shirts. I wore my cat costume, a real killer. I was down to my whiskers and G-string, on all fours on top of the coffee table, meowing and making them bark at me. I had them howling like farm dogs. But I misread them. Some clown pulled the light switch and said, 'Let's see if the pussy can see in the dark.'

"When the lights went on, they had my hands tied behind my back, and my G-string stuffed in my mouth. They bent me over the arm of the couch and smashed some seat cushions over my head to keep me quiet. Then they just held my legs apart and took turns at me. There were a lot of them, and some were really drunk, so it went on for a long time, and they had fun with it too, pouring drinks on me, poking around with ice cubes. When they were more or less finished, one wise guy stuck a maraschino cherry inside me and said, 'There, good as new.' It took a very long time. Did I say that?"

Darlene keeps her eyes stitched to Possum's. He's frozen in place, one hand on his cards, the other in his lap. She can sense Billy, Walter, and Roberto in the periphery, can feel their eyes on her.

"They left me like that, and when I finally managed to stand upright, the room was empty except for one really drunk slob sitting on the floor with his back against the couch between my legs. He was asleep with one arm around each of my ankles, holding on to my heels, his head jammed between my thighs. I kicked him awake and got him to untie my hands, but I was too tired and sore to do any of the things to him I now wish I had. So anyway, what do you say, Possum? Shall we raise the stakes? I mean, now that it's just you and me?"

It takes Possum a moment to snap out of it and realize she's talking about the game again now, that the story is actually over. He swallows hard and croaks, "What have you got in mind?"

Darlene fishes two twenties out of the front pocket of her jeans. She irons them out on the table with her fingers and sets her last four wire nuts on top of them. She pushes it all into the pot. "Call it a hundred bucks, and I'm all in. You up to that? It's all I have to bet."

She yawns like she's unconcerned about the bet, throwing her shoulders back to work out a kink in her spine. Possum is looking at her like she just offered him something altogether different, like he's about to lunge across the table for her. She glances at the others. Billy and Walter are actually sweating; their foreheads are beaded with droplets. Roberto wipes the palms of his hands up and down his pant legs, then does it again.

Possum reaches into the pot and extracts her earrings. "Wouldn't want you to go naked," he says. "But I'll cover the hundred." He licks three fingers and reaches into his shirt pocket for a thin roll of bills. He counts out the money and holds it over the pile. His hands are trembling.

"Call," he says, dropping the bills. He turns his hole cards faceup and shows the wild deuce he caught on the last card that gives him four aces. He's blinking more rapidly than Darlene would guess possible. One knee is going up and down even faster.

She arranges her four natural sevens side by side on the table and then, almost as an afterthought, turns her last card faceup. It's the two of spades. Possum turns a shade of red you'd want to see a doctor about.

"Five sevens!" Roberto says. "Five!" It's the first time he's raised his voice all night, and his accent has disappeared. "I don't believe it! She didn't even look at the last card!" Possum stands and slumps over the table, knuckles pressed into the Formica top, his mouth hanging open as Darlene reaches out with both hands and crushes the pot against her breasts. Billy and Walter find their voices and start hooting about the odds against two players catching a wild card on the end, the insane way she bet it. They are both humbled and deeply in love. Possum remains standing, looming over the table, incredulous. After a moment he drops back into his chair. "You win the deal," he says, pushing the cards her way. He won't even look at her.

She elbows the big pile of wire nuts and bills aside to make room for the cards. As she stacks and shuffles them, she wonders which will bring her more pleasure: telling him that he is such an oaf that he flashed that two of spades as he dealt it to her, or letting him believe—letting them all believe—that she pushed the bet like that without really knowing she had the five sevens. It's a tough choice.

"And let's keep the table talk to a minimum," Possum says. "No more stories, huh?"

"Sure, Possum. Whatever you say." She winks at the others.

She finishes the shuffle, offers the deck to Roberto, who declines to cut. She prepares to deal.

"So, what's it going to be now?" Billy says.

Darlene pretends to ponder the possibilities, but there's really no question in her mind. She feels great. And if Possum doesn't want her telling any more stories, that's fine with her. She doubts she could make up another one quite that good, anyway. A maraschino cherry? Where in the hell did that come from?

"Well?" Possum says. "Come on, name it." He's furious, absolutely quivering all over.

Hey, better him than her.

"Ante up," she says, finally. She undoes one button on her blouse, tosses her hair, and starts dealing the cards around the table. "Same game," she says. "Follow the Bitch."

A Girl, the Jungle,
Monkeys

————

It was Robert's first trip to Central America, and he had been there less than a week when the two angry nodules erupted on the back of his head. He didn't remember getting bitten or, for that matter, even seeing any insects around the lodge—other than the resident midnight roaches every time he turned the bathroom light on. But now, as he sat in the deep-hulled panga waiting for the local Garifuna boatman, Samuel, to cast off from the dock, the bites flared in fiery agony. Robert let out an involuntary yelp and rubbed the throbbing, grape-sized lesions.

Samuel leaned forward and pinched two fingers of Robert's hair, carefully lifted it from around the aching wounds. "Beefworm," he said. "Two a dem. Probably pick 'em up yesterday when we in de lagoon, looking on dem manatees."

"What?" Robert spun in his seat. "Worms?"

"Oh sure." Samuel flashed him a huge gold-capped smile. "Dat botfly lay his eggs on a cow, or dog, or a man. And when dey hatch, de worms dig right in and make demselves a little house in you, fix dinner! Down here, sooner or later, dey in most every living ting. Don't worry. Two or three months dey move on."

"You're joking," Robert said, as he massaged his scalp and studied Samuel's face, rufous brown in the pink dawn light. The man did not appear to be joking. "Two or three *months?*"

"Nah, you don't wanna wait with dat painful chewing on you. When we get back tonight, we'll put bacon on dem breathing holes. Worms poke dey heads out and we grab 'em. You got tweezers?"

"I don't think so," Robert said, trying to take it all in. Fly larvae burrowing into his flesh? Breakfast meat slapped on his head? He tried to stand but doubled over with sudden abdominal cramps that buckled his knees and dropped him back into his seat.

"What now?" he gasped as another savage shudder racked him.

Forgetting the stinging bites momentarily, he fished two Imodium tablets from his shirt pocket, ripped them out of their foil wrappers, and stuffed them in his mouth. What was he doing in this part of the world anyway? Adventure travel? Fuck adventure travel! He should climb out of the boat while he was still able, catch the next plane back to Belize City, and get the hell out of the whole damn country. Forget the stinking jungle trip. Forget the goddamn howler monkeys. Forget—

Then the young woman, Rachel, came flapping down the dock in rubber sandals, lobbed her backpack into the boat, and flopped down on the seat beside Robert under the shade bimini. She gave him a smile that could cure cancer.

And since the fly larvae weren't actually hurting him any longer, and since his intestines had more or less quit twisting for the moment, and since, apparently, there would not be anyone else joining them for the trip to the Spider River thirty miles down the coast, instead of getting out of the boat, Robert looked past the gently undulating coconut palms and saw the dawning sun, a blood spot above the luscious pink horizon. And he looked at the woman sitting next to him, bright and fresh and twenty-five years younger than he, and it really didn't surprise him at all that Samuel already had the boat planing away from the dock and through the soft, foam-flecked breakers before Robert even finished that thought about staying behind.

———————

He had met Rachel briefly the evening before at the lodge when his traveling companions, the Amundsons, had insisted she join them for dinner because she was American and so young and traveling alone in a strange country—never mind that these kids did that with a recklessness that verged on impunity, in Robert's opinion. But no one asked him, and anyway, he was supposed to be broadening his horizons a bit.

The Amundsons were not on board Samuel's panga that morning, would not be going down the coast or up the Spider River on the jungle trip as planned. They were already way past Imodium and well into the Cipro pills and the more immediate effects of Kaopectate and, when last seen by Robert, were laid out in their cabana, prostrate and whimpering with the particular kind of self-pity reserved for people whose expensive vacation has just been demolished by raging diarrhea. They insisted he go on the river trip without them.

Sprawled on her bed in her wadded, slept-in sundress, Mary Amundson moaned, "I gave my ticket to that girl Rachel. The kid has hitchhiked across Mexico, just spent a week alone in Guatemala. She'll look out for you, Robert." She gave him a dismissive smile, took a swig of Kaopectate straight from the bottle, and massaged her stomach. "Anyway, Theresa would have wanted you to go."

Robert glared at Mary, bristling at both the suggestion that he needed caring for and the presumptuousness of her claim to know what his dead wife "would have wanted." He looked at Mary's fine blond hair sweat-glued to her temples, the pink rime of Kaopectate at the corners of her mouth, the bottle clutched against her chest like a wino's last drink. He had the sudden murderous urge to raise his camera and snap one of her, just like that. But Mary was a very old friend, and anyway, what if she was right?

"Just me and the girl?" he said. "I don't know." But he did.

From the bathroom, Steve Amundson groaned, "Are you crazy? A girl. The jungle. Monkeys. Go, man. Go, go, go."

Mary closed her eyes and nodded.

Robert said, "I'll give your regards to the crocodiles," and he went down to the dock, feeling the tiniest pang of an impending cramp in his gut but refusing to acknowledge it.

———

Samuel had the boat running parallel to the shore and was two miles down the jungled coast by the time Robert realized he'd left most of his own medications in his cabana. Beside him, Rachel held her backpack between her knees as she unearthed a tube of sunblock. She was wearing a red two-piece swimsuit and, over that, a man's short-sleeved white dress shirt, open like a sport coat. She had a small gold ring through her navel and a tattoo of blue chain around one ankle. Robert watched her apply an oily sheen to her already tanned arms and neck. She squinted and gave him a crooked grin as she greased her forehead, nose, and cheeks. When she went to work on her bare thighs, he had to look away. Theresa had been gone for four months, and aside from the tear-sloppy hugs from female friends, this was the closest he had been to a woman since.

It wasn't too late to ask Samuel to turn back, but Robert felt the reassuring warmth of the sun pressing through the nylon shade bimini. The botfly larvae in his head were apparently sleeping. His stomach was calm. He fingered the last two Imodium tabs he had in his pocket and decided he would tough it out. Really, how bad could things get?

He glanced at the girl. She was nineteen or twenty, he guessed, thin, flatchested, and small limbed. She was dark, had an Italian-sounding last name he had heard at dinner but couldn't recall now, had black, boyishly short hair and a little trace of fuzz along her upper lip, and every time she swung in or out of her ever-present backpack, he couldn't help staring at the forests of her unshaven underarms. Her too-large brown eyes made her appear startled but attractive in a way that was new to Robert, or at least seemed new. And he was both horrified and delighted to discover that he was letting himself boil up a major crush for her. What the hell. It was a vacation in a strange land. His first time in the tropics. His first time anywhere without Theresa. And after all, some of Theresa's last words to him had been, "Robert, consider this a dying wish, OK? After I'm gone, please, have some fucking fun."

So when Rachel set one foot up on her backpack and spread her knees to smear the inside of her calf, Robert pretended to be fiddling with the lens cap on his camera and allowed himself just the smallest peek at the tufts of fine black curls sprouting from the edges of her swimsuit. After all, a dying wish was no small thing.

Finished with the sunblock, Rachel turned to offer him the tube but hesitated, and Robert was suddenly conscious of his long-sleeved (guaranteed UV resistant) shirt, buttoned at the wrists; his tan Ex Officio "trekking" pants, festooned with zippered pockets from hip to ankle; the light wool socks he was wearing inside his brand-new Tevas—the first sandals of any kind he had ever owned.

Rachel eyed his floppy, wide-brimmed shade hat. "Well, can't be too careful," she said, with no apparent sarcasm. She stowed her sunblock and offered a greasy hand. "Rachel," she reminded him, as if he might have forgotten.

He felt another queasy rumbling in his abdomen and wondered whether it was the same insidious organism that had flattened the Amundsons or merely the incomparable feeling of gliding across the Caribbean at dawn with a young woman's fingers in his palm.

"It's Bob, isn't it?" she asked, and he almost corrected her but managed to bite back the word *Robert* in time, flattered that she remembered him at all.

"Yes," he said. Then the two fly larvae in his scalp began gnawing their way through his subcutaneous fat and sent a jolt of pain clear to his ankles. As calmly as he could, he raised one hand to his head and ground his teeth in agony. "Yes, it's Bob."

Mercifully, Samuel shouted over the drone of the outboard, "One hour to Spider River. Maybe less." And as Rachel turned in her seat to dole out one of her smiles, Robert took the opportunity to dig his nails into the swollen fly bites until his eyes watered.

Rachel turned back to him. She put a hand on his shoulder, threw her head back, and took a deep, long lungful of sea air. "Isn't this great, Bob?"

There was that startled, literally "wide-eyed" enthusiasm again. Well, why not? She was young. What did she know of the possibilities for pain in this life? He managed a smile through the stinging in his head, the ominous churning in his bowels. "The best," he said.

And of course, it was. To the left, the blue, opaline sea stretched to the dawn-lit horizon. On the right, black cormorants dropped like swollen fruit from the low branches of the beach mangroves and began an awkward paddle-flapping race across the water. Above them, creamy white egrets burst from the foliage and into the cloudless morning sky. Needlefish and ballyhoo rocketed from the surface on each side of the boat, and a hundred yards ahead, a school of blue jacks churned through a soup of panicked bait. Rachel clutched Robert's arm, pointing excitedly as a squad of pelicans smashed bucket-mouthed into the melee. "It's such a bummer your friends couldn't come," she shouted over the engine.

"A shame," he said, snapping a photo of the birds but thinking about having the Amundsons there in the boat now: Steve and Mary, with whom he and Theresa had spent every vacation, every holiday, and probably two out of every three weekends for the past fifteen years. Steve and Mary, who only knew him as one half of the Robert-and-Theresa unit, now unmoored and pathetic. Steve-and-Mary-and-Robert-and-Theresa: It had become one word. He looked down at Rachel's fine brown fingers wrapped unselfconsciously around his wrist. "It's a definite bummer," he said.

By the time they arrived at the village of Spider River and Samuel snugged the bow of the panga up onto the mud bank next to a line of dugouts and wooden skiffs, the pounding of the hull across the early-morning swells had taken its toll on Robert's insides. Despite both the Imodiums and the heady pleasure of Rachel's company, he was thinking only about a toilet.

The sun was higher now, still climbing, and already white. When Robert stepped out from under the bimini, he was astounded by the staggering force of the heat. The fly larvae didn't like it much either, and he felt a new flash of flesh-ripping pain as the creatures began boring deeper into him. He mashed his fingertips hard against the throbbing lumps behind his ear and tried to stifle a groan, while Rachel sprang from the boat like an elf, swung into her backpack, and marched off into the village. "Come on, Bob," she called back over her shoulder. "Isn't it neat?"

"Neat," Robert said, weakly. He sat back in the shade, attempting to gauge the urgency in his spasming bowels as he waited for the larvae to settle down. "I'll be along."

The village was a cluster of tidy tin-roofed and clapboard-sided houses perched on stilts on a small floodplain along one side of the little river. In the shade beneath the houses, skinny dogs slept curled in complex tan knots; young black children played among stacks of wooden lobster traps, piles of net, rope, and conch shells. Between the houses, white chickens loitered in the sunny weeds. Beyond them, the jungle towered, fiercely green and ragged-topped, looming over the little settlement as if it were deciding whether or not to swallow it.

Still queasy, Robert sat in the boat a moment longer, vacantly watching a swarm of scuttling fiddler crabs pick its way across the steaming low-tide mud. He was about to ask Samuel for directions to a rest room when a sudden tortured shrieking erupted from the village, and he looked up to see a young local woman racing from the jungle. She was clutching a large green papaya under one arm and screaming horribly as she ran, swatting with her free hand at invisible attackers around her head. Three men scrambled to catch the girl, also swatting at whatever was tormenting her. Behind them came Rachel swinging her backpack madly and shouting, "Killer bees! Killer bees!"

For a moment, Robert thought Rachel had joined in some sort of game. But when he felt something crawling up his chin and, without thinking, slapped it, he received a searing sting on his lower lip that made him jump back in his seat as though he could get away from his own face. "Oh, Jesus!" he cried. This was all he needed. "Oh my God!"

Samuel already had the outboard roaring and slammed it into reverse, nearly pitching Robert from the seat as they plowed away from the river mouth and back out into the sea. They stopped a hundred yards offshore, engine idling while they watched Rachel and the three village men tackle the screaming girl and cover her with a canvas tarp one of them produced from somewhere. By then, a handful of other villagers had run up, brandishing burning palm fronds, and in a few moments they all stopped swatting and dodging their attackers, though the girl still lay on the ground where she had fallen. Everywhere now, small, smoky leaf and palm frond fires burned, and the whole village was soon shrouded in a blue-gray pall.

"Christ," Robert said, sucking his stung lip. "Is there anything here that *doesn't* bite?"

Samuel said, "It's why dey call it de jungle, man." He pushed the idling boat back into gear. "We better see about dat girl. She's stung real bad."

Back on shore, the girl who had brought the angry hive into the village was lapsing into unconsciousness, and Rachel was acting so nonchalantly about the half dozen stings to her own arms and legs that Robert couldn't bring himself to mention the painful swelling on his lip. He stood among the crowd of villagers surrounding the poor girl, fanning the acrid smoke away, and stared at the girl's fitful face—eyes swollen shut, lips ballooning, angry red lumps sprouting about her cheeks and neck. The girl's mother sat on the ground holding her daughter's head in her lap, the girl gasping for air as the swelling constricted her throat. Robert thought he knew all about trying to hang on to someone who was dying, but listening to the woman wailing in her incomprehensible Garifuna dialect, he saw that there was always room in this world for one more model of grief. In the grass at their feet, the big green papaya lay broken open. Blue flies skated across the wet orange pulp.

In spite of the heat, Robert felt a chill spreading across the back of his neck, his intestines sending him a message not to be ignored. He managed to pull Samuel aside. The nearest rest room turned out to be behind the Spider River police station, a squat, unpainted cinder-block building near the water's edge. Robert slipped away from the discussion of what was to be done for the girl. As he was about to round the corner of the building, Samuel shouted, "Check for spiders before you sit down, man!" Several of the villagers standing over the unfortunate girl nodded at the wisdom in that.

"Spiders," Robert said. "Oh, good." But he was sweating furiously now and going dizzy, and he was in no condition to look for creatures of any kind. Convulsing with chills, he muttered, "One more goddamn thing stings me and I'm going to blow my brains out." He hurled himself the last few yards to the toilet as the room began to swim.

———

Robert awoke some time later, stewing in sweat, lying on a cot in a tiny, suffocating shack with rough sawn walls and a rusted metal roof. Above him, upside-down lizards roamed the wooden rafters, lapping up God only knew what kinds of invisible insects. In places, there were nail holes in the obviously recycled roofing, and the strong midmorning light streamed into the room in hard white beams crowded with fluttering gnats. The door to the shack was ajar, and through the opening he could see a slice of the river, a glistening serpent in a world of dry green underbrush.

With effort, he lifted his head enough to see his pants and socks hanging over the back of a wooden chair at the foot of the cot, his camera on the seat, and his sandals on the dirt floor beneath it. He was still wearing his sweat-soddened shirt and, for some reason, his hat. A light cotton sheet covered his naked legs. He brought his hand to his chest, feeling for the soft cloth security pouch that dangled from his neck and contained his passport and most of his cash. Relieved to find his valuables safe, he tried to remember getting onto the canvas cot, but all he could recall was sitting on the toilet in the baking heat of the concrete-walled room behind the police station, watching a fiddler crab scratch its way in under the wooden door, and then another one and another after that. He remembered hearing their spiny legs clicking as they approached and briefly thinking that they were coming for him, icy sweat forming along his jaw line, and then sudden drowning nausea, the walls melting, the spalled cement floor lurching up at him.

A shadow fell across him, and he looked up to find Rachel in the shack with him. A ray of light from the punctured roof hit her face, lit the fuzzy hairs on her upper lip, and glinted in her navel ring. "You passed out," she said. "We found you on the floor. Samuel wanted to take you back to the lodge, but the boat was stuffed with that poor girl and her family. He says your fever should run its course, though he would love to get after those fly larvae you have camping in your head." She grimaced. "I think they put bacon on them."

"So I heard." Robert lifted one trembling hand to the swollen bites. His hair was matted to the lumps and his fingertips came away sticky with some kind of fluid. Jesus. Leaking sores, diarrhea, fainting. Had the girl come in to find him on the floor of that stinking room facedown among the crabs with his stupid nylon pants around his ankles? "I used to like bacon," he said. The bee-stung lip made his words thick.

She smiled. "Rest for a while. There was a flash flood last night in the mountains. It closed the road between Placencia and Dangriga. Samuel has to take the girl all the way up the coast by boat. He won't make it back before dark. We're staying over."

"Overnight?" Robert tried to sit up, but the ceiling ballooned down on him, the rafters torquing wildly. White lights flashed at the edges of his eyes. He eased back down. "I can't stay. My friends . . . "

"Samuel will explain to the Amundsons when he gets back from Dangriga." She put a cool hand on his forehead, and his whole body shuddered. "Relax." When she pulled his eyelids shut with two fingertips, the lizards on the ceiling disappeared. In their place, a feverish image of his dead wife wavered before him and vanished. He thought about reaching out for Rachel's hand, wasn't sure if he should.

"Look," she said, bringing him back to the world. "You need to stay lying down. Try to get some sleep. I'll be back in a few hours. I'm going to go upriver with a guy I met."

"You met a guy?" He heard the whine but was unable to stop it. "Here?"

He's alone in the jungle with a girl, and she meets a guy! Why didn't she just strap him to an anthill?

"Gunther," she said. "He's German. He's been living here in the village for a couple months, studying natural medicines. His teacher, an old local man, went in Samuel's boat with the injured girl, but Gunther says he can can fix up something herbal for you. Cool, huh?"

"Gunther," Robert groaned. "Cool."

There was a movement at the doorway. A tall young man in a stain-blotched FUBU T-shirt and ragged khaki cutoffs entered the hut. Backlit by the fierce white sunlight, he semed to be wearing a headdress of some kind. When he got closer, it was clear that it was only his hair, dread-locked and matted and lying across his shoulders in flattened bundles like so much dead grass. The sticky odor of very old sweat and something else clung to him; it was either marijuana or patchouli, and it depressed Robert immensely to think about how long it had been since he was able to tell the difference.

"Gunther," Rachel said. "This is Bob."

Gunther was about Rachel's age, athletically muscular, tanned, and too handsome for his own good. He wore a bracelet made of woven hair and a huge yellow tooth or claw of some kind on a thong around his neck. Robert thought he might have to hate him.

In perfect, unaccented English, Gunther said, "Rachel tells me you're feeling puny." He smiled as though that delighted him somehow.

Robert was definitely going to have to hate him. "I'm much better now," he said.

"Not." Rachel shook her head at Gunther. She said, "Can you help him?"

"I can make some craboo leaf tea for the diarrhea, some special roots I know for the bee sting. Of course, nothing works like bacon for the botfly maggots." Gunther explained how the creatures would be enticed to crawl partway out of Robert's head when the bacon was held on their breathing holes, the necessity of pulling out each larva intact. "You break off a segment inside you, it will go septic fast in this heat."

Robert groaned and waved for him to stop.

"Bob's right, we should go," Rachel said. "He needs to rest." To his amazement, she bent back the brim of his hat and kissed him on his fevered forehead. "I'll see you tonight." She and Gunther disappeared out the doorway.

"Tonight." Robert let the word linger on his lips, not sure what, if anything, that meant, but liking the sound of it very much. Cautiously, he eased up on one elbow and watched them walk toward the river. Gunther said something that staggered Rachel with laughter, and she hung on his elbow. He threw his arm across her shoulders with a familiarity that was a poison dart in Robert's chest.

As if on cue, the botfly larvae went on the rampage again, and the pain sent his intestines twisting once more. He willed himself to stay calm, whimpering quietly until everything had more or less stopped aching. From the direction of the river, he heard Rachel's laughter again, and then an outboard started up. He listened to it shift and drone away upriver as he watched the lizards overhead doing upside-down pushups and considered the silliness of his feelings for her—for God's sake, she was just a girl, and he hardly knew her. Just a girl, just a girl. A girl.

The boat was gone, and in the silence he tried to sleep, but the sticky citrus smell of fruit rotting somewhere nearby filled his nostrils, and he was suddenly coming through the door of Theresa's first apartment above De Tonio's Produce, and they were both nineteen and tipsy on Harvey Wallbangers, the drink that was the rage on campus that year. They began tugging at each other's clothes before they were all the way through the door, still in the kitchen, fumbling with buttons and zippers and giddily declaring in lubricious detail exactly who and what was about to be kissed or licked, and so on. When they heard the loud "Ahem!" from the adjacent living room, it took them an awkward moment to remember that Theresa's mother had mentioned stopping by for a visit—and that she had her own key. True to their natures, Robert went immobile with shame, and Theresa fell to the floor and laughed so hard she actually wet herself.

Wallowing in the memory of Theresa's youthful carnality, Robert found—amid all his aches and discomforts—that he had an erection and had his hand on it, and that he had the urge to masturbate. But even through the fever, he knew that if he gave into it, he would do so thinking not of Theresa but of Rachel—who was a quarter century younger than he. And he was appalled. Was he becoming an animal? It was a good question, though it didn't make him any less hard.

His feelings for Rachel drifted into thoughts of Steve Amundson, who found it necessary to regale Robert with tales of his student conquests at the university where he taught. "Everyone is studying women these days," Steve would say, grinning. "I'm just doing the hands-on research!" Then, in social situations, Robert would have to watch Steve dote on his wife, Mary, as if nothing were going on, as if Steve were the most solicitous, loyal, and caring husband in the world.

Thinking about lies and secrets, he was once again in Theresa's hospital room in the last days of her life. While Theresa drifted in and out of tortured sleep, he watched the television up on the wall, the set tuned to the Home and Garden Channel where she wanted it—as though she would ever get to paint another window frame or plant another flower bed. Over the soft background murmur and hum of the hospital, Robert listened to a woman on the screen wearing a lab jacket and discussing common yard and garden pests: aphids, leaf miners, tent worms, slugs. When she used the word *infestation* Robert involuntarily glanced at Theresa's ravaged face. Theresa had not been paying attention to the TV, and apropos of nothing Robert could see, she said, "Tell me one thing you've kept secret from me all these years."

"A secret?" Robert tried to make a joke of it. "My osso buco recipe?"

"I'm serious. There must be something you haven't wanted me to know." Then a little more quietly she added, "Adults keep things from each other, even people they love. It's natural."

Theresa's face was unreadable, had been for days, ashen and slack, weary beyond hope. Not even the nuns were talking about hope by that point. And though Robert was never one for picking up on subtle clues, it occurred to him there was a reason she had brought up the subject of secrets.

"You first," he said.

She hesitated, seemed to think about it. "Robert, you're like a child in some ways, and after I'm gone, I don't want you blundering along with an unrealistic memory of me. So I'm just going to come right out and say this."

Robert had sat there, so stung by the accuracy of her assessment of him that he barely heard her say that she had been having an affair with a man she worked with. That it had gone on for months and months, at a time when Robert would have sworn that everything was perfect in their lives and that they were both happy and contented together. She had broken it off only after she was diagnosed. And Robert's face burned with pure humiliation for once again being shown naive and unworldly. Because being considered childish was something a man could laugh off. But being thought *childlike* was another matter altogether.

Stunned, Robert said, "Why would you possibly tell me this now?"

And she looked at him coldly and said, "Because *you'll* live, Robert."

He was once again mortified at the way he was always being surprised like that. And when she insisted that he take his turn and tell his secret, he found that he had nothing remotely on the level of an infidelity to balance out the scales with her, which seemed to further confirm his immaturity and angered him even more, and so he told her this: "When we lived in the house on Carson Street and we kept Cody and Moose in the pen behind the garage, remember how that gray cat next door used to walk along the top of the fence and drive them nuts and make them howl? Well, one night one winter, we came home from the movies or some play or something, and it was late and dark, and you went into the house straight from the garage, but I went out to check on the dogs, and when I turned the yard light on, the dogs were standing at their gate wagging their tails and very excited about something. And so I went to the gate to give them some attention, and at their feet was the gray cat, almost torn in half, with his head crushed in and one eye hanging out."

He regretted it immediately, of course, actually winced as Theresa's shoulders slumped in despair beyond pain. He had told her not just because she loved all animals—even that cat, which she thought was clever and bold for tormenting a pair of hundred-pound malamutes—and not just because she couldn't stand to see an animal injured or suffering and nearly wept at every road-killed creature they'd ever driven past. He had told her this, almost fifteen years after the cat had been secreted in the garbage can and the dogs were long dead, because she would never have imagined that her sweet and loving pets were capable of such monstrous violence, and so it was her turn to feel naive. And now she was hurt too. And so they were even.

Only, as Theresa had pointed out, she was dying and he was not.

———————

When two Garifuna children raced by the door, shoving each other and screeching playfully, Robert became aware that he was still in the hot little shack. He lay there a moment, trying to clear his head of the guilt-swamped memory of ending his life with Theresa in an exchange of cruelties like that.

In a daze he swung his feet over the edge of the cot and rocked himself upright, wiping his eyes on the backs of his shirt sleeves. Another lurch and he was on his feet, hanging on to a low roof rafter as the room whirled around him and the lizards scattered across the metal ceiling. The botfly larvae in his head went crazy with the sudden movement, and this time he didn't even try to stop the cry that escaped his swollen lip. Sweat poured from him, coursing down his ribs as he clawed at his buttons, tore the sopping shirt from his back, and stepped out of his damp undershorts.

He was at the doorway then, clutching the wood frame, swaying limp-kneed, half out the opening, trying to focus on the green blur of vine-strangled foliage surrounding the village. Somewhere out there was whatever happened next.

Hours had gone by somehow, had escaped his fevered awareness, and now the sun lay impaled on the spiny jungle treetops as Robert staggered out of the shack and into the shimmering late-afternoon heat. He took a step toward the forest, and it erupted with the hoarse screams of the howler monkeys, the taunting shrieks of toucans and macaws. Village dogs bayed and yelped insanely, and the green jungle air pulsed with the deafening drone of a hundred million insects. At the riverbank, the girl and the ganja-smoking young German with the bongo dreads appeared, waving bunches of ceiba, craboo, and cohune leaves and calling out to him. But as he plunged into the thorny underbrush—ghost white and naked, except for his hat and his pouch of valuables—all Robert heard were the botfly larvae drilling into his head, the amoebae roaring through his gut, and the endless hollow pounding of his heart.

Water of an Undetermined Depth

I found what I was looking for in the morning paper: A boy had fallen from the roof of an unfinished building and been impaled on a steel reinforcing rod. The metal had punctured two chambers of his heart and nicked his jugular vein, yet the kid did not bleed. "One in a billion," his doctor was quoted as saying. The boy was listed in satisfactory condition—although I couldn't imagine what might be satisfactory about a child with a hole through his heart. But I did draw some comfort from it all. I would like to believe that kids today are incredibly difficult to kill.

My daughter Lucy shifted her weight from foot to foot as she watched me set the newspaper down on the table. "Well?" she said. She had her bathing suit on, her towel draped over one shoulder, a tube of suntan lotion in her hand—on her face an expression that came as close to patience as a fifteen-year-old can be expected to muster when dealing with an obtuse parent. Her friends were out in the driveway waiting with the engine running. They were going swimming at the quarry. Lucy said, "Dad, come on. Say it's OK."

Truth is, I wanted her to go. Kids should have fun. God knows there's time enough for pain and sadness in this life. But I wanted it to feel all right to me, too—no small order. If Lucy's mother were still here, it would have gone like this: I'd say, "Absolutely no way, Claire, it's too fucking dangerous." And my wife, Claire—the realist of the relationship—would line out all the logical reasons that it was in fact as safe as just about any-thing a teenage kid would care to do. Claire would shake her head and say, "You can't hang on to them forever, you know." Then after some more squirming, I'd give in and Lucy would go swimming and I could rest assured that if anything (God forbid) happened, I had tried to tell them. On some level, of course, I knew that Claire was right about not being able to hang on to someone forever. But I didn't know she was talk-ing about herself.

Lucy said, "Dad, Carmen is going to run out of gas in our driveway if you don't hurry."

What I really needed was another of those lurid tales of barely averted tragedy. That last one, the one about the boy with the rebar through his heart, that was a good one, a doozy, one in a billion for sure. But that quarry was deep, and Lucy was as thin and bony as an anchor.

I considered telling her about the teenage boy in Montana who had been accidentally shot in the neck while hunting with a friend. Somehow, according to the papers, the bullet managed to miss all the big arteries and his windpipe. It came to rest in his mouth. It cost him a few teeth, a couple of stitches. Maybe he had to have his jaw wired. I couldn't remem-ber much except the comment from the hospital spokeswoman: "Let's just say the word *miracle* has been used a lot around this place today."

Sooner or later, you have to ask yourself, Am I the kind of person who will get to use that word someday? Well, there's a reason they call them miracles, and it isn't because they happen all the time.

Lucy said, "Hello! Earth to Dad! Come in, Dad. Can you read me?"

I told myself that hundreds of children swim in that quarry every summer without incident. How many drowned, really, when you added them all up? Even so, this called for more than mere logic.

"The quarry?" I said.

"The quarry," she said, almost but not quite amused by my stall. "You know, Dad. Rocks? Water? People having fun?"

A story came to me about a nine-year-old girl in Louisiana who had fallen into a sinkhole full of snakes—cottonmouths, or water moccasins as the locals call them, but poisonous as hell just the same. The little girl had spent the night in this pit full of vipers and been bitten more times than anybody cared to count. There was a picture of her in the paper, and her skinny little legs looked like someone had worked them over with an olive fork. A local herpetologist said, "Enough poison in this kid to drop a steer." But here's the really good part: She had no reaction to the venom. None.

Lucy was sucking on her teeth, twisting her towel into a tight knot. We both knew that this request was just a formality, that I couldn't possi-bly refuse her this. Not for the first time, she was willing to take her mother's role in the little farce. "No fooling around, Dad," she said. "No diving. And we'll come straight home after."

If I'd asked her to, she would have sworn this in a blood oath. And her eyes said that she truly meant it and really believed that she would behave in this responsible fashion. Still, I knew that she couldn't keep such a promise and that she shouldn't have to, either, that it was a promise made not to be broken so much as forgotten, a promise that, in the heat of the afternoon, would slip away and vaporize into the summer sky or slither out into the middle of the quarry and sink out of sight. She said, "You trust me, don't you?"

What could I say? That it wasn't exactly *her?* That it was a matter of judgment, and the way judgment seems to vanish whenever two or more teenagers gather beyond the sight of adults?

"Who's going to be there?" I tried to sound neutrally curious.

Even as I pursued this line of questioning, I could see the flaw in it. I couldn't know everybody, every time. And kids don't only learn from others. Someone has to set the example. There must be ideas that simply spring to them as fresh and original as Descartes' first meditations. The first kid to walk the railing of the railroad trestle, the first one to put a .22 rimfire cartridge in his father's workbench vise and tap it with a hammer, the first one to dive from the ledge of the quarry into water of an undetermined depth. Somebody has to be first. Still, I can't help thinking that a lot is taken from example.

I fabricated a quick drowning story for Lucy. It was about a kid named Tommy Ciccio I had grown up with. In the story, Tommy and I are down at the Niagara River at the end of our street. It's Easter vacation. The day is sunny, the elms just starting to bud. Lake Erie has broken up, and the river is jammed with huge planes of sheet ice, dirty, gray, and treacherously honeycombed. Tommy steps off the dock behind the cement company and balances himself on a flat sheet of ice the size of a grand piano. He is smiling, laughing, having too much fun to acknowledge danger in even its most obvious forms. He is calling to me, telling me to try it. But I've already got a soaker, and the wind off the river is cold against my wet pant leg. I turn away and walk home, leaving Tommy alone with the river.

Lucy seemed to buy it. I told her that when I looked back once more, Tommy was waving good-bye at me, that the river never *did* give his body up. In truth, Tommy Ciccio is a locksmith in Fort Lauderdale. I figured it wasn't the worst lie a man could tell his daughter.

Lucy presented her own case. She was an excellent swimmer. There would be dozens of kids at the quarry with her, hundreds of people swimming. There were no waves. There was no undertow, no current. There would be no rough stuff. It was a safe, public place.

I had to admit that she did a good job—she was going to be the lawyer of the family. And I knew that I couldn't stall her much longer. If only I had a little more reassurance, some small comfort to sand off that last edge of uncertainty about this whole thing. As Lucy concluded her final argument, I scanned the paper once more and finally found what I'd been looking for. Second section, inside page, lower left: LAUNDROMAT EXPLODES. A young girl in New Mexico had slipped a dime into a gas dryer and turned it on. The explosion blew out one whole wall of the building, broke windows across the street, and rolled a car over onto its side, but the girl suffered only minor bruises and the loss of her eyelashes. "You just can't figure it," an official with the state troopers said.

No, you can't.

Lucy had turned toward the door.

"Wait," I said.

There was another story that the laundromat piece brought to mind: the day my best friend Henry Dukovski and I built the snow fort. But that was my story and mine alone.

It was a day off from school, a snow day. The city plows were way behind schedule. The neighborhood was lost under a sea of snow, and Henry and I dove into the drifts as if we could swim in the stuff. We flapped onto our backs, spread our arms and legs and became angels, rolled the snow into balls as big as boulders.

The snow fort was Henry's idea. We built it waist high against his house where the dryer vent spewed warm, bleach-smelling exhaust into the gray afternoon air. "Heat, man. We got the only heated fort on the block," he said. We rubbed our mittens together under the steamy exhaust for a minute before stacking the last of the huge snowballs in place. Then we dragged a sheet of plywood from the alley where Mr. Capoletti stored building supplies. We slid it across the top of the snow fort walls to form a roof. Another small scrap covered the doorway.

We stood back, surveying our work. I was sweating. I let my scarf flap open away from my neck. My mittens were soaked. My pants were soaked. My boots were packed with snow. Henry was completely encrusted from his chest to his ankles. If it bothered him, he didn't let on. He began packing snow around the plywood, stopping up the leaks where the dryer exhaust seeped out from under the wood.

I told him I was freezing, that I wanted to go home. I started walking toward the front of his house.

"Hold on! I got a surprise for us. Unbelievable too," he called out. His eyes were wild. He looked like a little Russian elf.

The last "surprise" Henry had produced was his father's service revolver. He let me hold the gun, spin the cylinder, even pull the trigger on an empty chamber. I wasn't going to miss action like that.

"I'll be right back," he said. He disappeared inside. When he came back out again he was grinning madly, winking theatrically, as if poked in the eye with a stick. He herded me toward the snow fort.

It was snowing again, the flakes clotting into wads the size of communion wafers. Henry stopped just outside the fort. He opened his coat. Tucked in the front of his pants he had a big chrome flashlight and a magazine that was rolled up as tight as a window shade. On the cover I could make out the head and naked shoulders of a woman.

"Oh," I said.

"You bet," Henry said. He laughed.

We scuttled into the snow fort. The temperature outside was twenty-five degrees, but within the thick snow walls we had to take off our mittens, our coats. Mrs. Dukovski must have done laundry all afternoon. The steaming exhaust from the dryer never stopped. The walls were glazed with melting snow, the floor hard-packed and slick as newly waxed linoleum. Steam condensed and froze on the plywood ceiling in stubby icicles, furry with lint. The only sound was the steady pinging of a zipper against the metal drum of the dryer in Henry's basement. We sprawled on our coats and opened his father's magazine. Henry directed the flashlight at the photos.

By today's standards, it was pretty tame stuff. Upthrust bosoms, rigid nipples, bared bottoms offered with a back-over-the-shoulder smile of a sort I'd never seen in my thirteen years.

Henry flipped the pages as I gaped, overheated and sweating. I ignored the water dripping from the plywood overhead, the creeping cold radiating up through the ground under our coats. A wad of lint wafted down and came to rest on one woman's rump. I thought about picking it off but hesitated to touch even a photo of that.

"Look," Henry said. He had unzipped his pants. His hand moved up and down. "Try it yourself." He looked more elflike than ever. "Go ahead!"

Of course I tried it, and a few minutes later, when the results caught me by surprise, I thought I was breaking down, melting. The air inside the fort was suddenly unbearable, the bleach fumes suffocating.

"Henry," I cried. I scrambled to kick out the door, yanked at my coat, partially frozen into the ground. When I tried to stand, I hit my head on the plywood roof, now thoroughly cemented to the walls by the frozen snow.

"You didn't tell me, Henry."

"What did you think we were doing it for, dupa?"

I crouched in the doorway, tucking myself back into my snow-soaked pants. I felt like a fool. "I'm wet, " I said. "I'm freezing." I tugged at the front of my flannel shirt.

"Go home then," he said. He looked around the close space, sleepily, as if he'd just awakened from a dream. He looked at me in the doorway. He'd been lying directly under the vent and his head was covered with lint: red, blue, gray, and white. Little clumps of it stuck to his lank blond hair, his eyelashes. "Go. I'll take care of myself," he said. He turned back to the magazine. "Fix the door," he added, without looking up. "And remember, this is a secret."

"Henry," I said. "Who am I going to tell about this?"

I put the cover over the door and went home.

Around nightfall, a howling Canadian storm front blew into town, dropping the temperature to zero and below. When Henry failed to show for dinner, the Dukovskis assumed that he was at my house because we played and ate and slept at each other's indiscriminately. By the time they phoned to tell him to head for home, it was very late. Too late for Henry.

I wasn't with my father when he helped Mr. Dukovski heave the snow-covered plywood off the fort. I was huddled in my warm bed, already wondering if I could make that strange little explosion happen again. But in the years to follow I would hear my father tell the story a hundred times, and he would never fail to describe Henry with all the colors of the laundry lint glazed into his face. "A clown," my father would say. "He looked like a small, frozen clown."

Startled by the sound of car doors slamming out in the driveway, I looked up from the newspaper to find Lucy gone from the room. I heard a car accelerate and fade off into the distance.

I must have said, "OK, honey. Go ahead. Go, but be careful." I certainly said, "Be careful."

In any case, she was on her way, and I felt a sudden chill run along the backs of my arms, down my legs. I found myself pacing the floor of my empty house, hands in pockets as if to warm them, as if it weren't eighty-five degrees and humid, a beautiful summer afternoon.

At the open window of our dinning room, I stopped and looked out at the neighborhood. The street was quiet now, nothing moving, no one in sight. In the maples along the driveway, cicadas began their powerful and relentless whining, like some monstrous household appliance—a vacuum cleaner in agony, a can opener gone mad. In the distance, I heard children, doing childish things.

Old Friend

———————

The week before I got out of Gambler's Rehab Ranch, my wife, Katie, left me, closed our bank account, and took a waitress job in Bullhead City; the day after I got home from the ranch, my father moved in with me. I don't know if this is a coincidence, but it was also right about that time that I started hearing voices from the poker room.

My father and I live in a small two-bedroom apartment now, here in Las Vegas on Salton Street, three blocks east of the Strip and virtually in the shadow of the big casinos and hotels. Dad has been sick with one thing or another for as long as I can remember and also had a major nervous breakdown about a year ago when my mother died. After that, my sisters decided that since I had made it through rehab—twice now—I must be fit to care for him. What they really meant was that since Dad had accidentally burned down the house we'd grown up in after forgetting to pay the fire insurance on it and had moved his pension funds and the cash from my mother's life insurance into an investment scam in Nigeria, and since (unlike my sisters) I had no spouse, no children, and no career, I was the one who got Dad.

I think it's safe to say that nobody aspires to be living with his father in an apartment the size of a storage unit at the age of forty-two. And I guess I could be bitter about my wife going south and my inheritance ending up in deepest Africa. But realistically, if you live in Vegas long enough, sooner or later you are bound to lose something.

Dad watches a lot of TV now, though his watching is mostly listening. On top of his other problems, he has such severe, inoperable cataracts that the TV screen, like everything else in this world, is only a blur to him. At the Safeway checkout one day there was a little canister with a slot in the top for donations to something called "The Change a Life Foundation." Dad bent close and squinted at it while I paid for the groceries. "Change of life. There's a good cause," he said. "Hot flashes. Your mother suffered like you wouldn't believe." At her memory he started bawling right there in the store. He didn't even want to play the video poker slots by the checkout line, a little diversion I allowed myself since I had renounced table games (if they knew about this at rehab, they would have a cow). I had to take him home. And me with two rolls of quarters in my pocket just screaming for action.

Dad likes the sound of the TV and leaves it on all day and all night. It's his world now—that and the bathroom, where he spends an unbelievable amount of time too. But mostly it's the TV. Sometimes I'll walk in and find him sitting there in front of the set with his lids clamped shut and I'll say, "Are you sleeping or awake?" Dad will open his eyes and say, "Does it make a difference?"

The voices from the poker room come through the television.

It started a couple weeks ago. Maybe it's some glitch in the cordless microphone they use in the casino to call people on the waiting list for seats at the tables. All I know is Dad had the sports channel on, was sitting on the couch in his pajamas, nodding off, waiting for me to fix him some lunch, and in the middle of a Mexican soccer match, over the drone of the announcer and his endless statistics, I heard Tommy, the poker manager at the Mirage, say, "Attention ladies and gentlemen, we have seats available in the poker room. One- to five-dollar Seven Card Stud. And five- to ten-dollar Texas Holdem. Seats open in the poker room."

His voice was as clear as if he were right on the couch next to Dad. I dropped the grilled cheese sandwich I was about to flip and ran to look at the set, expecting to find Tommy there in a TV ad promoting the casino. But on the screen all I found were hundreds of Mexican sports fans flooding out of the stands and onto the field as the terrified referees ran for their lives.

This sort of thing would never happen if Katie had still been here. I said, "Dad, did you hear that?"

My father blinked. "Sure," he said. "Four to nothing, Veracruz. How's that sandwich coming along?"

I called Mel and Bob.

Mel and Bob are the owners of the Gambler's Rehab Ranch up near Ely, where I've done two different stretches trying to quit poker. Mel and Bob themselves claim to have been millionaires before they lost it all to gambling and found Jesus. It might be true, who knows? In rehab, it's critical that you believe what they tell you, or you don't stand a chance. Bob is a big red-faced Texan who laughs every time he speaks, as if he's discovered just how silly life is and can't hide it any longer. Mel, his wife, is a tiny little cowgirl, thin as a rope, weighs maybe a hundred pounds carrying her heaviest Bible. She laughs almost as much as Bob does. It's a kind of therapy they use. At the ranch there is at least as much merriment as depression. That's something I can't say about gambling itself, which, in my experience, is very rarely funny.

Mel answered the phone, and I told her about the voice from the poker room. "He said, 'seats available,' Mel. I swear I heard it come from the TV."

She didn't laugh, and neither did Bob when he took the receiver from her.

"You better get back up here, son," Bob said. "Mucho pronto."

I had to take care of my dad, I told him.

Bob said, "Son, the Devil's got your number, your zip code, your shoe size."

For some reason, Bob's pithy pronouncements weren't as compelling over the phone as they had been at the ranch. At the ranch, once you made the big step of declaring that your gambling was a sickness and not just a factor of you being a fuckup all your life, everything Bob and Mel said sounded so right. But now . . .

"Maybe I heard wrong."

"He's got your picture in his wallet," Bob said. "He's playing your song on his jukebox." He still wasn't laughing. "Remember, you can't bluff Satan, son. He don't bet unless he's got the nuts."

Mel took the phone from him. She offered me a discount rate if I'd check back in immediately. They really did try hard, I'll give them that. I said I'd think about it.

I hung up, retrieved lunch, and sat on the couch next to Dad and tried to eat my sandwich while I kept an eye on the TV. The Mexican soccer had been replaced by a kayak race. There was no further sign of Tommy from the poker room, so I flipped through the channels, vaguely thinking about the Mirage Hotel and Casino: that pretty little waterfall, all those palms and bromeliads, the tropical tranquility of the huge saltwater aquarium behind the front desk, that wonderfully hokey gas-fired volcano out front. And yes, I'll admit, the big beautiful poker room. But on every channel I turned to there was just the usual mindless midday television.

I said, "Dad, I have to go back to work now."

Because I had left behind more than a few flaming bridges in my various poker tailspins over the years, I didn't have a lot of prospects when I got out of the ranch this last time. Mel and Bob found me a job at a Christian gift shop owned by some friends of theirs. Selling "What Would Jesus Do" bracelets didn't pay much, but the owners let me go home to fix lunch for Dad, and I'll tell you, there aren't a lot of people in this town half that nice.

Before I left the apartment I said, "You know the rules, right, Dad?"

"Yeah, sure," he said. "No stove."

"Right, no stove, no hibachi, no barbecue. I'll fix dinner when I get home."

Dad focused on me as best he could. What little hair he had, stiff and white, was all mashed over to one side and sticking straight out over his ear, as though he'd been out standing in the wind. He said, "I wish your mother was here."

I said, "I know, Dad. I wish I still had *my* wife too."

As I was going out the door, I heard him mutter, "This is no fun at all."

The next day we were eating breakfast at our TV trays on the couch when it happened again. Dad had just gotten up and found his way to the bathroom, and I was working through my bowl of cereal, watching Bryant Gumbel, when Bryant's mouth opened and out came the slightly Asian and lilting feminine voice of the graveyard manager at the poker room, Bao. "Ladies and gentlemen, we are starting a five-ten high-low split Omaha game at table number six. High-low split, Omaha. Benny, Lance, and Victor, take your seats at table number six, please. All players welcome."

I sat there stupefied. Bao was a great-looking Thai woman with glossy black hair down to her tailbone and a smile as sweet as rolled up aces. Back when I was playing six nights a week, I developed a terrible crush on her. One morning, after a night catching cards you wouldn't wish on your ex-wife's lawyer, I had a cup of coffee with Bao in the casino coffee shop and almost took her up on an offer to go home. But I needed to get back in the game, needed to get even again, and said, "I'm married. I can't."

"You guys," she laughed. "If you were up a couple hundred right now you wouldn't be able to tell me your wife's first name."

"Katie," I said. "See?"

Bao smiled and shook her head. "Doesn't count. Anybody knows his wife's name when he's losing."

Again Bao's voice came out of Bryant Gumble's mouth. "Benny and Lance and Victor, to the poker room, please."

I felt my pulse surge. Benny and Lance and Victor were three live ones, retired dentists from Palm Springs with more money than card talent, and three of the surest pigeons a real player could hope to find in this lifetime. It was 9 A.M., and they were trying to get up a game of Omaha, which none of them understood at all. They'd have been up since sometime the night before and would be tired and anxious and making the kinds of sketchy plays you go to your grave regretting. All a guy like me would have to do is slide into that game fresh with eight hours of sleep . . .

My father returned from the bathroom. There was a big round wet spot on the front of his pajama bottoms. I decided it was too late to ask him if he needed help.

"*Now*, I can eat," he said, lowering himself into his place on the couch behind his tray.

I said, "Dad, I have to open the store."

I got up and put my bowl in the sink, thinking about how many hours at $6.50 per hour I'd have to work to raise the stake I'd need for a five-ten Omaha game, thinking about how much I could clear in a morning at a table with marks like Benny, Lance, and Victor. I mean, if I were still playing. If I hadn't quit.

I reached for the front door and was about to remind my father of the rules again before leaving.

"Yeah, yeah," he said. "No stove, no matches. Listen, I was thinking, in there on the pot. You could call your wife."

"And say what? That I've been home for three days and haven't gone back to the game yet? That will impress her."

"All right, don't bite my head off." He stuck another spoonful of cereal in his mouth and said, "It was just a thought." A trail of milk trickled down his chin and dropped onto the front of his pajama top.

I said, "Dad, while you're thinking, why don't you think about getting dressed today. I mean, if you're not too busy. And throw those damn pajamas in the hamper so I can take them down to the laundry room!"

I slammed the door and was halfway to the store, still stewing about that easy-picking Omaha game I was not going to see, before I realized what I had done. So I called home when I got to the store and got no answer. I worried about Dad all morning and felt exactly like the shithead I am.

When I came in at lunch, Dad was sitting in front of the TV in the same place he'd been when I had left, but he was dressed now, and shaved, and had combed most of his hair, and he looked very nice, almost handsome, in his baggy old-guy jeans and plaid cotton shirt. I was still feeling awful for having snapped at him, but my apology had to be put on hold, because sitting next to him on my couch, intently watching Maury Povich interview a lady with a parrot on her shoulder, was a huge red-bearded man I had never seen before in my life.

"This is Dewane," Dad said. Neither of them turned away from the TV. "He just got into town last night."

"Dewitt," the large, bearded man said, finally peeling his eyes off Maury Povich. "Name's Dewitt."

"Oh yeah, Dewitt," Dad said. He squinted at the screen, trying to make out what he was looking at. "Is there something on that woman's shoulder?"

"Some kind of a bird," Dewitt said. "A cormorant, I think."

Dewitt was huge, almost twice the size of my father, with beef-slab shoulders and hands the size of catcher's mitts. He was young, maybe thirty, though bald with bushy red-orange eyebrows the same color as his chest-length beard. He wore a black knit shirt, thin to the point of transparency where it stretched across his massive belly; brown and gray camo-patterned nylon pants with cargo pockets up and down the legs; and black loafers over once white socks. Though my father obviously couldn't see it, Dewitt had a face that said, "Dial 911."

Dad said, "Dewitt here is going to break the bank. Those casinos are in trouble like they've never known. Right, Dewitt?"

"I do feel like a winner," Dewitt said, folding his hands across his belly.

"So, Dad, where did you and Dewitt meet?"

"Dewitt was sleeping in the laundry room," Dad said.

"The laundry room." I kept my voice even as I crossed to the kitchen area and opened the fridge. "What were you doing down there, Dad?" Then I remembered the stained pajamas. "I would have done the laundry."

"I don't believe in hotels," Dewitt said. "Who knows who's slept in those beds?" There was a trace of something East Coast in his voice. "What things they've done on those sheets." Let's face it, this guy's voice made you think, Where are his meds and why isn't he taking them? He said, "You have any idea how much radon hotel carpeting emits? How many fluorocarbons?" His eyes were all but throwing sparks now. The top of his head was glossy with sweat. "I don't even want to talk about oxidants," he said.

The thing was to remain calm.

"Right," I said. I took out the mayonnaise, some lunch meats, bread. "Will you be staying for lunch, Dewitt?"

The question hit him sideways. He glared at the kitchen counter and clenched his enormous fists like he was about to come up out of his seat. I prayed that whatever alien transmissions he thought he was receiving wouldn't order him to carve my father and me into hand puppets. Then, as quickly as it had come over him, the tension passed and he unclenched himself. "No mayonnaise for me," he said calmly. "It feeds the cancers."

"Hold the mayo for Dewitt," I said.

"Cancer," Dad said. "My wife . . . " He bit his lip and looked up at the ceiling with his sad, cloudy eyes.

Dewitt said, "The doctors won't admit I have it. They think they can keep it from me." His eyes sparked up again, and he pursed his lips and started making little huffing sounds through his nose.

"No mayo for Dewitt," I said, putting the sandwiches together.

Dad patted Dewitt on the knee. "Those doctors are something else."

Once again Dewitt grew calm as fast as he'd gotten hot, and while he and Dad compared medical stories, I made lunch, determined not to set him off again. On the TV, Maury Povich talked to the woman with the parrot on her shoulder. The woman, I guess, did something nice for animals, because Maury just finished saying to the audience, "Isn't she a truly wonderful human being?" when I distinctly heard Tommy at the Mirage say, "Bruno, Rico, Mario, Lolo, and Wendel. Your table is ready. Ladies and gentlemen, we have a ten-twenty Texas Holdem game starting up. Seats available."

I spun around from the kitchen counter to see if Dad and Dewitt had heard it, but they were still discussing the shortcomings of the medical profession.

"I do all my own diagnosing now," Dewitt said. "It's really the only sure way."

Dad nodded knowingly. "My cataracts? I saw them coming before anyone."

Dewitt seemed steady enough at the moment, so I brought their lunches in and set them on the trays. I stood with mine watching the TV, waiting for more from the poker room. There was a commercial for some type of family van, a little bullet-shaped thing stuffed with smiling children and their happy parents zooming along a lovely tree-lined road somewhere out there in that other world where "cards" meant Crazy Eights and Go Fish. The man was driving; the woman was in the front seat gazing at him as though buying that automobile was the smartest thing she had ever seen a man do. But the voice-over was Tommy saying, "Bruno, Rico, Mario, and Lolo, your table is ready." Then it was the jazzy car ad music again.

I stood there with my sandwich in my hand, shaking my head. Bruno, Rico, Mario, and Lolo? In one game? Are you kidding me? It would be feeding time at the shark pool. And some guy named Wendel was going to play ten and twenty Holdem with all four of them? Wendel!

Why didn't they just carry the poor bastard out to that volcano and throw him in?

I heard Dewitt say something that made me turn away from the TV.

"That's right," Dewitt said around his sandwich, "they don't want you to know this, but you can do your own X-rays if you can find a big enough Xerox machine." He held one finger upright before my father's nose. "I also figured out a way to give myself a prostate exam. You lie on the floor on your back and put your legs—"

I said, "Dad, Dewitt probably has to get going."

Dewitt shrugged. "Not really." He had slipped his shoes off and looked very comfortable there on the couch. "Do you have any more of these pickles?"

On the TV, that carload of happy people raced off toward the horizon, and Maury Povich reappeared, smiling, ready for his next guest.

───────────

The first time I came back from rehab, I actually thought I was cured. So did Katie. I needed a day job, of course, but after playing cards for so many years, I didn't have enough on my résumé to recommend me as a dishwasher. And, as with every place in Vegas, you have to drive right past the casinos to get to the unemployment office. Needless to say, it wasn't long before I was at it again in a big, big way.

I couldn't let on to Katie, obviously, so I told her I had found a job painting houses in a new subdivision west of town. I would go out the door each morning in my white pants and spend the day playing Hol-dem. At four o'clock I'd show up at home as if coming in from work. On Fridays I'd hand over forty hours' worth of wages to Katie, who handled the household money for obvious reasons. All weekend I would try to stay interested in whatever she and I were doing while I gnawed my nails wondering what I was missing at the game.

This went on for months, and for the first time in my life, I was actually having a streak. Then one Saturday morning I was lying in bed when Katie walked into the room wrapped in a towel, hair all wet and stuck to her neck and shoulders, fresh from the shower and looking so beautiful and sweet it made me forget I had ever seen a poker deck in my life. She said, "The kid is here to collect for the newspaper. Do you have a couple dollars?" I, not paying attention, said, "In my pants on the chair." And she reached into the pocket of my whites and came out with $9,260, and that was the end of that.

At Mel and Bob's rehab ranch, they said that, subconsciously, I *wanted* Katie to find the money, wanted to get caught. What I really wanted, of course, was for Katie to sit behind me at the game in a chair that the floor man had pulled up just for her. I wanted her to sip from a bottle of Evian and look over my shoulder in awe while I pushed a wired pair of kings all the way to seventh street, for her to reach out and lay a gentle, adoring hand on my arm as I raked in the chips and slid the dealer a tip too big to believe. But at rehab I just nodded my head and said, yes, I probably did want to get caught. You know, unconsciously.

When I snapped out of my daydream, Dad and Dewitt were still on the subject of their various ailments.

"Irritable bowel," Dewitt was saying. "That's another thing."

"Tell me about it," my father said. Suddenly he stood up. "Gotta go." He headed for the bathroom, leaving Dewitt and me alone.

I glanced at my watch. They'd be looking for me at the store. I checked out Dewitt's eyes, and either he was doing better or I was getting used to them.

I decided to take a chance. I said, "Dewitt, I'm glad you could stop by for lunch, but my father needs to get some rest this afternoon. His nap?"

Dewitt seemed to ponder that a moment, eyes swirling again with that weird mix of ominous concentration and pure, deep emptiness that left you wondering whether you should give the poor guy a hug or just start running. He nodded as though he'd come to a decision, stood, and slipped his shoes on.

Then he reached into one of his huge pants pockets.

OK, I thought, this is when he pulls the knife out. It's nine inches long, and he hones it daily on the jawbone of the last man who hadn't wanted to spend an afternoon discussing Dewitt's imagined tumors. I thought, this too my wife will somehow blame on my gambling.

Out of Dewitt's pocket came a huge wad of bills. He had nine or ten rubber bands binding the roll, and he started prying them off and carefully stretching each of them around his meaty wrist.

"What do I owe you for lunch?" he said.

I stared at the roll. Even if they were all small bills, there had to be a couple hundred, minimum. And the face on the outermost bill did not look like George Washington's.

I said, "My treat."

Dewitt pulled himself up to his full six feet plus. His shirt rode up, revealing a wide slice of pink belly and the frayed elastic hem of his yellow-white briefs showing above the top of his pants. His beard was sprinkled with sandwich crumbs and bits of salami. He said, "Do I look like a man who needs charity?"

I glanced at his money roll. "Not at the moment," I said.

"How much?" He peeled off a fifty and was reaching for the next bill. I checked to see if he was kidding, but it was clear that whatever other quadrants of his brain were still functioning, the one that managed the counting of money had burned out. "How much?" he said again.

There was a joke all the old lounge comics in Vegas used to tell. It went like this: A guy is walking down the street and bumps into an old friend with a history of gambling problems. The old friend immediately starts up: His wife's in the hospital, he's behind in his car payments, the gas has been turned off at the house, his children are hungry. Can the guy help?

The guy is no fool. He says, "If I give you money, how can I be sure you won't use it for gambling?"

The old friend shakes his head. "You don't understand," he says. "I *have* money for gambling!"

"Come on, really, how much?" Dewitt said. He was skinning big, beautiful, greasy bills off the roll and holding them out to me uncertainly.

On the TV, Tommy's voice cut through the talk-show chatter. "Would the ladies with the Organization of Retired Catholic Lay Teachers who wanted to learn to play Texas Holdem please report back to the poker room. We have a table ready for you now."

Retired schoolteachers?

"You have to tell me." Dewitt was begging. "If you just tell me how much, then I'll know."

This is what I learned at poker: Skill means little, and luck even less. What you need is talent, and I mean the talent to sense who at the table is on shakier ground than you; who is down to one eye, one kidney, one lung.

Maury Povich stood to welcome his next guest, while Tommy's voice said, "And all you nice folks who attended this morning's beginners' class on Seven Card Stud, we now have seats available at our one- and five-dollar tables."

"Is this enough?" Dewitt thrust a fistful of cash at me. He was starting to twitch, but there was none of that dangerous anger now. This was pure tortured confusion. "Is it enough?" Clearly he had no idea.

The casino was filling with amateurs, pigeons, fresh trout—people from places where they still leave CD players in unlocked cars and where children walk to school without bodyguards. It was filling with guys who smile at you over the poker table like it's a campfire, guys who give you the feeling that they have never in their lives resented the frailties of a parent, never had truly compelling reasons to deceive their wives.

Dewitt stared at the money in his hands. Fat, glistening tears began to roll out of his eyes and down into his beard. "Please," he whimpered. "Tell me what's right."

If he went anywhere near the casinos, they would hoover that money out of him before he finished telling them about his homemade MRI.

I said, "I'm thinking. I'm thinking."

From the bathroom I heard the toilet flush, then my father yelling, "I forgot to tell you, your wife called!"

And on the TV, Maury Povich looked straight into my eyes and said, "We have seats available in the poker room. We have seats available."

Winter Fish

The room was dark when Peter opened his eyes, and for a moment he lay drifting in the blackness until his wife's familiar breathing beside him shaped itself into the fact that he was in a motel room in Aztec, New Mexico, and was to meet his guide at the river at eight that morning. He raised his glowing watch dial to find that it was 4:10 A.M., and he wished he didn't know that he would not be going back to sleep.

As he began to ease out of bed, his wife spoke from the darkness. "I was hoping you'd make it through the night," she said. Her ability to detect his slightest waking movements was so unnerving that he was ready to believe she could hear his eyelids roll back. "I mean, what with the plane, and then that horrible, long drive, I really thought you'd sleep."

She was right. It had been a tiring trip, starting with four hours in the air from Anchorage to Seattle with an infant squalling all the way. Peter had watched the baby's mortified mother pace the aisle of the plane, her eyes glued to the floor as she shifted the wailing child from arm to arm, hip to shoulder. The woman, pale and too young for motherhood, reminded him of someone, but he couldn't put his finger on it. When the woman looked up to find him staring, she said, "It's the pressure. His ears. He can't help it." And Peter, caught off guard, had blurted out, "I'm going fishing," as if that explained anything.

Then, driving up from Albuquerque in the rental car, they'd hit a blizzard on the east slope of the Divide, a storm worthy of any he'd seen in all his years in Alaska, and a startling side of the desert he'd never imagined. It was the week before Christmas, the temperatures in the twenties across the entire Four Corners region. Plowed snow lay clumped like cottage cheese along the road through the Jicarilla Apache reservation. The sandstone cliffs were striped with white, and the sagebrush and junipers bent under its weight like so many old men staggering across the desert. "We could have stayed home for this kind of abuse," he had said to his wife. There were fingers of ice on the puddles in the motel parking lot, but at least the San Juan was open and fishable. At home the rivers had been frozen for two months.

Peter rolled out of bed and felt his way to the small, round pedestal table under the window. A cool draft oozed out from behind the rubbery motel window drapes. He groped around in the dark until he found his hooded sweatshirt hanging over the back of the chair, pulled it on.

"Will this light bother you?" He located the bead chain on the hanging lamp and gave it a tug. The bulb threw a cone of sickly yellow light onto the tabletop.

"It's fine," his wife said. Even so, she pulled her head under the blankets.

"I'm going to tie a while then." He set the portable kit on the table, removed the little vise and attached it to the edge, spread the packets of feathers and fur across the Formica. He fixed his reading glasses on his nose.

His wife rolled back the covers, squinted at her watch. "Not too long," she said. "You'll need some sleep. If you're going to fish all day, you'll need sleep."

"Not long," he said. "I'll be all right."

She studied him. "You thinking about Janice again?"

He shook his head. He continued to push the fly-tying materials around on the tabletop, setting the little plastic packets of feathers to one side, the dubbing furs to the other, lining up the various spools of yarn and floss and thread in no particular order.

"She has to make her own mistakes," his wife said. "She's twenty-one years old."

"I know."

He tried to sound unconcerned. He knew she was still watching him. He slipped a spool of waxed thread into the bobbin and concentrated on threading it, sucking on the end of the thin stainless-steel tube until he felt the thread uncoil against his tongue. Then he set the bobbin down and began rattling through the plastic hook boxes. The sound drove his wife back under the covers.

Now I'm thinking about Janice, he thought. *Thank you.*

Peter's daughter, Janice, hadn't told him about the baby, but news like that seemed to have a life of its own—and it loved to travel. Janice hadn't told him much of anything lately, hadn't called him in over a year, he realized—now that he was thinking about it. She lived back East with her mother, Peter's ex-wife, and he was well aware of how busy she might be, a young person trying to get a foothold in this world. Well aware. And now this: a baby. Peter was astounded by the way Janice spoke of it so cavalierly when he'd called. "What about school?" he'd said. "Your career?" He heard the anguish in his voice and then realized he couldn't even remember what her major was. "I'll miss a couple of semesters," Janice had said. She hadn't sounded concerned.

"What's the big deal?" his ex-wife had said to him. "I was younger than that when we had Janice." As if *their* foolishness justified their daughter's somehow! Was Janice to spend her youth working crap jobs? Languishing in unemployment lines the way they had? Is that how family traditions started? Had everyone gone crazy?

Peter forced himself to set the subject aside. He knew better than to get started thinking about such things at that hour of the night; the familiar burning sensation was already beginning to climb his gullet. "Esophagitis," his doctor had said. "Really hammers you at night, am I right? Keeps you up?" The doctor smiled, pleased to have guessed correctly. "It's quite common in people your age." He wrote a prescription.

People his age? Peter wasn't wild about being lumped in with a whole generation of medicine-swilling insomniacs. He never got the prescription filled. Now he wished he had something to cool the fire.

He considered going out to look for a carton of skim milk, some Maalox, but he had no idea if there was anything open that late in the strange town. When they'd pulled in the evening before, they'd stopped for dinner at the Aztec Restaurant, and he realized he was the only man in the place not wearing cowboy boots. He had looked out into the parking lot and seen the little rental car surrounded by battered pickups and flatbed farm trucks and would not have been surprised if he'd found horses tethered there. Who knew if these people stayed up late? They probably had early-morning chores to do.

He pushed the idea to the back of his mind and clamped a number four, long-shank streamer hook into the vise and started in on a huge black Woolly Bugger and felt better immediately, calmed by the familiar tension of the thread against the hook, the soft give of the marabou feathers between his fingers. He felt himself relax as he wrapped the chenille for the body and then palmered the hackle and tied it off. The ease with which it all came together comforted him. He was pleased with the way it looked, although it was not a pattern he would be using that day on the San Juan. The outfitter had made that clear enough.

"These are winter fish," the guide told him over the phone. "They're cold and slow and focused on the really small stuff. Size twenties, even as small as twenty-twos. Diptera, chironomids, maybe some small *Baetis* if it doesn't get too sunny."

Peter had heard the smug, more-technical-than-thou tone, the almost laughably serious way these young guides talked about their rivers, their fish—as though they had a handle on what was truly important in this world. He knew there was a time when he had been that certain about things, but he couldn't imagine now what any of them might have been.

"Really small stuff," he said to himself as he finished wrapping the head of the enormous Woolly Bugger. "Give me a break."

He always started with something big on these middle-of-the-night tying jags. That was his cure for the insomnia: start with something big and simple—streamers and leech patterns, steelhead flies—then work down to the small drys and nymphs. Work down, shutting out everything but the details, working smaller and smaller until nothing existed but the hook and the thread and the feathers, and they all got smaller and smaller and smaller until they just disappeared. Until everything disappeared. That was the secret for sleep.

When he was done with the Woolly Bugger, he held it up to the lamp. It was fully four inches long, thick, and heavily dressed. It could pass for a small bird. He smiled at the thought of lobbing something that size at these precious midge-sipping rainbows. He found himself wondering again what he was doing there at "The Juan," as the guide had called it.

Should he have gone back East instead of coming down here to fish? That had been nagging him. But to what end, really? The baby was on the way. It was done. Who knew what Janice was going to do now? She had gotten by somehow without him this far.

The wall heater unit kicked on with a clank and aroused him from his reverie. He glanced at the hump in the blankets that was his wife. She didn't fish, but this trip was her idea, her gift to him, really—and New Mexico had sounded good. It was only December, and already back home in Anchorage (with still five months until the season opener), his tying desk was overflowing with flies. The dogs had them stuck between their shaggy toes. The cat was spitting up feathers from birds it had never even seen. Morning after morning, Peter's wife was waking to find him hunched over the vise, bleary-eyed, a pile of feathered hooks mounding up in front of him. "We have to find you a place to fish winters," she'd said. "This is making you nuts. It's making *me* nuts." She'd gestured toward the front yard, lost under three feet of snow, as if that were his problem.

"And why is this winter so bad?" his wife had said. "It's no worse than usual."

"You're right," he'd said. "It's about average." He'd left it at that.

What *was* it about this year? Summer and fall had been the same as ever. The salmon came and went as always, and the leaves fell, and the river dropped and slowed and began to freeze. As always. And when he had finally looked up from the tip of his rod, finally taken his eyes off the surface of the river, he'd found that the ground was suddenly blanketed with snow and that fishing was over. There was nothing new in that; it happened every fall. And yet somehow he had known that this time, this year, winter was *really* starting.

Peter shook his head to clear it. His wife was right; Janice was a grown woman. She had a life of her own, and, if he had to be honest, that's the way he had always wanted it. It had been convenient, all those years and all that distance, the not knowing. The truth was, you could miss your children terribly and still be grateful, too. The trick was not letting the guilt kill you.

He set the big Woolly Bugger aside and clamped a number eight hook in the vise and tied a small Muddler Minnow. He took his time, making a job of spinning the deer hair onto the hook, then clipping it into the flat, sculpin silhouette those Katmai trout liked in June. After that, he tied a smaller stonefly nymph, a couple of simple caddis larvae. He was wrapped up in it then, working down to a size eighteen Yellow Humpy that was one of the best he'd ever done.

"OK," he whispered to himself. Though his whole body shuddered through a long yawn, he kept on tying, trying to keep his thoughts on the hook and the feathers and nothing else.

But still his mind wandered, and he thought about how often he had fished by himself, all those years, the predawn walks to the river through the still-dark willow thickets with the fear of big coastal brown bears pounding through his blood, the glorious morning hours before the sun chased the trout from the shallows where they fed on the smolts and sticklebacks, those beautiful afternoon hatches when the wind off the glaciers drove the fluttering caddis in horizontal sheets like a midsummer blizzard. And all those evenings spent casting at the mouth of the river, the volcanoes Iliamna and Redoubt blue against the red western sky across Cook Inlet, the salmon moving in waves around his feet and on upriver as though he were nothing but a minor obstruction in the stream. All those things he had seen, alone. It was not the cozy, two-guys-in-a-rowboat sort of picture people had of fishing. Was that what he loved about it? The distance it allowed him from everyone and everything? Or was it just the time it burned up?

He wished he could shut his mind off at times like this. Is this what growing older meant? Having that many more things to avoid thinking about? No wonder old people never slept. He wasn't even fifty. By the time he retired, he'd be shopping for a lobotomy.

He looked up from the vise. The details of the room were lost in shadow. He pulled back the drapes and peered out. A big semi sped by on the interstate next to the motel, the red taillights winking around a bend in the empty road. Peter glanced at his watch. In another hour it would be time to leave for the river. His heartburn had passed, and he thought about eating. He would stop and get some breakfast on his way, maybe one of those warm sopapillas with honey they served in the Mexican places. The thought made him happy. He let the curtains fall shut and put another hook in the vise.

Out of nowhere, it suddenly dawned on him who the young woman on the plane from Anchorage, the one with the crying baby, reminded him of. It was Hartley's daughter! Peter couldn't remember the girl's name, but there was something about the woman on the plane, her eyes maybe, so dark and tired, that reminded him of her.

It was so long ago. He couldn't have been more than fourteen or so. Hartley's daughter was just a child—eight or ten. She was a beautiful black-haired girl, like Hartley's wife, who was an Indian from up in Canada someplace. They were fishing the Wiscoy, in the hills south of Buffalo, Peter and Hartley and Hartley's daughter. Hartley worked at the graphite plant with Peter's father, and he had taken Peter hunting and fishing for a couple of years when Peter's numerous brothers and sisters kept his father too busy for luxuries like that.

It was spring, and the Wiscoy was running high, and all day as they fished, Hartley had to stop and carry his daughter across the deeper, faster runs. It was cutting into his fishing, and Peter offered to carry the girl when Hartley's patience was obviously running out. She was skinny and bony, and when she climbed onto Peter's back and swung her legs around his waist, he felt stronger than he'd ever felt in his life. He charged across the Wiscoy with her shrieking into his ear. They were both still laughing when he stepped into the hole. Afterward they sat in the warm spring sun, pouring water out of their hip boots and laughing some more.

Peter saw the girl once again, about ten years later. He was at his grandmother's house in the old neighborhood one winter evening when her upstairs tenant came in through the common hallway. It was Hartley's daughter, a young woman then, maybe nineteen or twenty. She had a baby on her hip, all bundled up against the cold except for his little hands, which were bare and bright pink. Peter recognized her at once, though she was very drunk and had no idea who he was, and she looked at him as if he were an idiot when he tried to remind her of the day on the Wiscoy. After she had reeled away and gone upstairs, Peter's grandmother said, "No gloves on the baby. Again. In this weather." She shook her head and rolled her eyes toward the ceiling. "All kinds of things going on up there." She sighed and gave a small, very Old World shrug with her mouth and hands that seemed to mean, "What kind of people neglect their own children?"

Peter shook the memory off and tried to concentrate on the fly tying. He was beginning to feel the lack of sleep now. Two more small dry flies, and his eyes were aching, the insides of the lids seemingly coated with sand. There was a numbness spreading along the back of his skull, across his shoulders, and down his arms. When he reached for the box of the tiny, number twenty-four midge hooks he'd bought in Albuquerque, it slipped through his fingers and bounced on the table. He pushed back the exhaustion he felt tugging at his heart, picked up the box again, and pried it opened. He had never seen anything so small. The hooks looked like tiny doll eyelashes, like crumbs of steel wool. The wire was so fine he couldn't feel it between his thumb and forefinger as he tried to position one in the vise.

"Winter fish," he said out loud. He took off his glasses and rubbed his eyelids and pictured steely bright trout finning across fields of snow, schools of them cutting through drifts that swelled like waves. Winter fish, leaping for invisible winter insects hatching right out of the icy snow crust. The fish were blue and cold. Blue trout on white snow. It was the coldest dream he'd ever dreamt. When he opened his eyes again, he felt giddy, dizzy with something almost like joy, and when he heard his wife's voice, hoarse with sleep and close behind him, he thought he was imagining things.

"What are you doing?" she said.

She was standing over him, her hands resting on his shoulders. He knew that should have startled him, her sneaking up and touching him like that. It should have put him into orbit. He never even felt it.

He looked up at her. She was squinting hard at the vise. "There's nothing in there," she said quizzically. She reached over him and ran one thin fingertip across the jaws of the vise. "No hook."

He leaned closer and peered at it. She was right. He searched the tabletop for the little hook, but the surface was cluttered with scraps of fur and feathers. Everything was beginning to blur. He reached for his glasses.

"Time to fish," he said, though he wasn't sure why.

"Listen to me, Peter." She was talking very slowly, very deliberately. "She is going to be all right." Gently, she pried the glasses from his grasp. "Can you hear me?"

He was still trying to figure out where the hook went, what he was supposed to do next, but was dimly aware that his wife had him on his feet, turning him away from the table. She was peeling the sweatshirt off him and guiding him to the bed. He knew that too, and he saw that the covers were turned down and that the sheet was a field of snow. He felt himself easing into it, and then the chill of the snow against his cheek, and he heard his wife say, "There really isn't anything you can do for her right now." And as he sank among the fish, he wondered—but only briefly—who in this world she could be talking about.

Love A, Love B

The afternoon sleet was clotting into snow as Bailey stepped out of the Safeway with a pumpkin in his arms and a woman named Jill on his mind. He frowned at the darkening sky. Halloween day and snowing, and he'd hoped they would get away without it just this once.

As he stepped off the curb, a Subaru wagon slowed to let him cross the icy pavement to his car. He nodded to the driver, a woman, who, though she looked nothing like Jill, reminded Bailey, like everything else lately, of Jill, Jill who was his lover, his mistress—whatever they called them these days. Girlfriend? Could you say girlfriend with a straight face when you were fifty-six years old? What did it matter? She was on his mind once more as he bent to set the big pumpkin on the front seat of his car and realized he'd forgotten the candy he was also supposed to buy. He slumped against the door frame and pressed the heel of his hand to his forehead. He had been like this for weeks.

Back in the store, he was turning to leave the candy aisle when he spotted the devil costume on the bargain table among the witch hats and skeleton suits. He set down the two bags of bite-sized Hundred Grand bars he was carrying. His wife, Ann, had instructed him to buy Snickers as always, but he liked the idea of something different this year. He reached for the costume.

On his drive home from the store, Bailey honestly tried not to think about Jill, who was three hundred miles to the north at a pump station on the pipeline that the company they both worked for operated, which was where they had met when Bailey was there on inspection and where he wished (for the hundredth time that day) he was again now, with Jill, instead of stuck in Anchorage with his wife, a pumpkin, and two bags of candy.

To keep his mind off Jill, he turned on the radio, but she had tuned it to the college station and they were playing some sort of ska music, or reggae, or maybe it was zydeco—he was never sure what he was hearing on her stations—and in the face of the escalating snow squall hurling itself against his windshield, the exuberant tropical rhythms were more than he could bear. He hit the button for the public station, where they were interviewing a very old woman somewhere in the Everglades who was earnestly explaining how she was trying to save "soon to be lost forever" recipes for possum and raccoon. "Small Things Considered," Bailey muttered, and turned the radio off again. "Dull Things Considered."

He glanced at the package on the seat next to the pumpkin. It was the first adult costume he had ever bought, and he told himself he was getting it only as a treat for his grandson David, who was three and would get a charge out of seeing Bailey in it. That made him think of Chenowith, who'd come to the office that day made up as a wizened old man, complete with Einstein eyebrows and a mustache the size of a white rat. Chenowith had spent the day rolling his eyes at the young women in Engineering and feigning senile lust, to the amusement of the whole floor. Well, Bailey thought as he slid into his snow-slicked driveway, he could tell them all a thing or two about lust. They would not believe it. NPR should be interviewing *him*, for Christ's sake.

The house was dark and cool, and Ann wasn't home. The elections were only a week away now, and she'd be working the phones for her candidate as they put the final push on. Bailey set the big pumpkin in the sink and dumped the candy bars into a metal bowl for the trick-or-treaters who would soon be coming. He laid the costume on the counter. There was a note from Ann propped against the Cuisinart. "Marinate the halibut at 5:00. Will be working at headquarters until 7:00 or 8:00." There was no signature. He looked at that briefly, thought about other notes, other years, how they had once finished them "Love, Ann" or "Love, Bailey," how that had dwindled to "Love A," or "Love B," or even just "A" or "B." That was to be expected, of course. In thirty years you expected a certain amount of dwindling. But not signing at all?

He wondered again if Ann suspected anything, because the affair with Jill was a first for him, and he had no way of judging whether he was hiding it well or whether it was tattooed in red and blue across his forehead the way it felt whenever he faced her. He doubted she knew. She'd take it hard. There would be more to deal with than unsigned cooking instructions if that were the case. Still, it had to happen sooner or later. As thrilling as that thought was, it also made his chest ache, and he put it out of his mind. He looked at the costume again. He pulled it out of the package.

The label said it was made in Sri Lanka, and it was called the Red Dragon, but anyone could see it was a devil. There was a full bodysuit of red nylon knit, over the top of which there was a stiff and scaly red rubber breastplate that attached under the arms. The cowl had spongy red horns; the body had a long, arrow-pointed tail. Then there was the mask, a ghastly black and red thing with small, almond-shaped eyeholes and a mouth opening that featured a red rubber tongue that lolled from the bottom lip. Something about the face looked faintly reptilian, and Bailey thought David was going to love it. He stuck the halibut steaks in the marinade and fixed himself a Jameson's.

He had his drink while he gutted the pumpkin into the disposal, making a job of scraping out the stringy pulp until the big spoon came up with nothing but stiff curls of pale yellow pumpkin meat. Bailey's pumpkin carving used to be a major family event. His daughter Kate, when she was still a child, made him bring his creations into her classroom. Even now, grown and raising a family of her own, Kate expected Bailey to carve one for her son, David, and Bailey was glad to. More than glad.

Instead of a jack-o'-lantern, this year Bailey decided to carve the silhouette of a spider on a web. He had seen one like that in the window of the Nordstrom store. It was far more complex than anything he'd ever attempted, but since this thing with Jill, anything seemed possible. And in fact, it came out so well he had to set a candle in it and turn out the kitchen lights. It gave him a rush of pleasure that almost embarrassed him, and—not for the first time—he thought that he should have gone to art school. How many engineers did this world need, really?

He looked up from the pumpkin at the darkened kitchen. The shaky candlelight threw unstable shadows across the dark oak cupboards. The faucet dripped, and above it, through the window—which had lost its seal and was fogged and fingered with frost—Bailey could see icicles stabbing down from the eaves, and he knew that ice dams would soon be forming on the overhangs and that the roof would leak once more. The place was falling apart. Just recently Ann herself had said, "Everything around here needs upgrading!" And Bailey had looked away.

He sipped his whiskey and considered whether that's what he was doing. Was it simply a case of replacing old with new? Or was it as silly as he feared it was going to look when it all came out? How was a man to know?

There was a knock at the front door. He thought with joy that it was his daughter and grandson there to pick up the pumpkin, and he wished he had gotten into the devil suit. But it was just a group of tiny costumed children, bundled up in winter clothes and wearing cartoon animal masks, so he gave them each a Hundred Grand bar, and they thanked him noisily. At the end of his driveway, two women wearing snowmobile suits and smoking cigarettes waited for the children. One of them held a baseball bat at her side. Bailey waved, and they waved back, their cigarettes etching orange tracers in the dark air. It was still snowing. He closed the door and went for the costume.

The devil suit was tight over the bulge in his midsection, and the horned cowl fit snugly around his face, but standing in front of Ann's door mirror, he was pleased to see how substantial the shoulder pads made him look. He turned and saw the long, stiff tail sticking out behind him. It made him smile. The only question was footwear. He surveyed his closet floor in despair: all those fussy oxfords, those wing tips. In the end, only the brown loafers seemed remotely right for it. When he slipped the mask on and faced himself, he had the sensation of being introduced to someone he had always wanted to meet.

He went back to the kitchen and fixed another whiskey and sipped it through the mouth hole of the devil mask, thinking about Jill again, of course, until another group of trick-or-treaters arrived at the door, older than the first batch. Everyone commented on Bailey's costume as he handed them their candy. That pleased him, but it was fully dark now, and Kate and David should have been there by then to pick up the pumpkin. He decided to call.

"Oh God, Dad, I forgot. I can't believe I forgot the pumpkin!"

Kate told Bailey that her husband had taken little David to a party at the Baptist church they were attending these days, a huge place with an auditorium that seated thousands and featured two giant video screens that offered everyone a view of the preacher's face at all times.

"At the church?" Bailey said to Kate. He was on the phone in the candlelit kitchen. "Isn't Halloween a little pagan for them?" He had long ago given up trying to avoid stepping on his daughter's religious toes. She changed beliefs often, each one a little further from her Episcopalian roots. Ann once suggested that it was Kate's way of "shattering the nest," a term she'd gotten from a book she had been reading around that time. He wondered now if Ann would find a book with a name for what he was doing to that nest.

"It's a harvest season party," Kate said. "To give thanks for the Lord's bounty. They have cider and punch, some Bible study too. It's so much safer than going door to door."

"Our door is safe," Bailey said. "Always has been."

"Oh, Daddy. I'm sorry. You sound miserable. Is the pumpkin good? It is, isn't it?"

"Museum quality," he said. He thought about his grandson at the church. Leave it to the Baptists to put a biblical slant on Halloween.

Kate said, "Maybe we'll bring David over later—if he's not too tired. You know, after the party."

She didn't sound very convincing. He stared at the pumpkin again. The spider seemed to hang there, suspended on thin strands of pumpkin flesh. He wished Jill was in town to see it.

"Daddy, are you listening to me?"

There was a loud hammering at Bailey's front door. It echoed through the quiet house, but he made no move to answer it. The phone line crackled.

"Dad?"

"Have to go, Honey," he said. There was more pounding at the door. "Got goblins out front. Sounds like big ones."

"Are you OK, Daddy?"

The knocking stopped. Bailey leaned into the hall and saw figures racing away from the front porch. In the nervous pumpkin light, his horned shadow sprang along the hallway wall.

"Daddy? You don't sound like yourself."

"Trust me, Kate. I know me, and this is definitely him. Bye, Honey." He hung up.

As he knew it would be, the porch was empty. On the storm door glass someone had scrawled in soap BLOWJOB.

Back in the kitchen, he drank his drink leaning against the counter. *Daddy.* He'd always liked the way Kate called him that. But she was what, twenty-five? God, Jill was only twenty-seven. Twenty-seven! In the elevator at work recently he'd heard two of the young geologists talking about women and sex, and specifically at what age a woman was best at it. They glanced at Bailey, and maybe because he had recently taken to dressing in turtlenecks and the cashmere jacket Ann had given him for his fiftieth but that he had never worn until he met Jill, they apparently felt that he could bear the subject, and one of them said, "Twenty-seven. Absolute optimum age. Old enough to know what they're good at, but not bitter about it yet." He grinned at Bailey, and Bailey—although appalled—gave him a look he hoped indicated that he knew plenty but wasn't saying.

The furnace kicked on, and warm air rose from the floor vent. The spider on the pumpkin quivered as the candle flickered. Bailey looked at it carefully. It really was quite good. It was terrific. Someone should see it.

He finished the last of his whiskey and picked up the pumpkin from the counter, set the bowl of candy bars on the front porch, and locked the door behind him. There was a group of small hoboes and clowns coming up the driveway as he was backing out, the pumpkin on the seat beside him. The candle went out, and the car filled with acrid, sooty smoke.

The Baptist church was an enormous sandstone edifice with a parking lot the size of an airport. Bailey got out of the car, straightened the mask, clutched the big pumpkin against the breastplate of the devil suit, and headed for the church, nearly losing it at one point when his slick-soled loafers hit a mound of ice. Snowflakes swirled gaily in a block of friendly light flowing out the glass doors and down the steps, but he had gotten no farther than the threshold when a small, taut woman stepped in front of him. She had high cheekbones and a chisel for a chin and impeccable silvery blond hair that gave Bailey the impression she'd had it professionally coifed every day since birth. She cut him a toxic stare.

"Excuse me," she said. She tilted her head, trying to see inside the devil mask, and gave him a smile that could have frozen oxygen. "Are you supposed to be here?" It was not a question.

Bailey looked beyond her but could see no sign of his grandson. People had caught wind of the confrontation at the door, and a crowd was forming behind the fierce little woman. A large white-haired man in a flannel shirt and bolo tie wrapped his fingers around the woman's upper arm as though he might lift her up and hurl her aside if needed. Looking straight at Bailey, he said, "We're right behind you, Marvelle. This kind of malarkey has got to stop."

Bailey said nothing, the thought suddenly occurring to him that there might be certain kinds of behavior too difficult to ever explain, and that showing up at a church wearing a devil suit and carrying a pumpkin with a spider carved on it probably fell into that very category.

A young man in a "Son Worshiper" T-shirt stepped to the front of the crowd. "The Lord looks through your mask," he said. He had pale blue-white eyes, which he closed as he spoke. The others watched him, waiting for his next pronouncement. Bailey opened his mouth to say that he only wanted to find his grandson, but the young man said, "He looks through *all* our masks."

Bailey thought, Is there anyone who didn't see that coming?

There was a chorus of amens.

"Maybe I've made a mistake," he said, and turned away.

"A mistake?" The young man's placid voice drifted down the steps behind Bailey. "He knows all about mistakes." More murmuring from the crowd.

Bailey kept walking, thinking of his grandson among these people. As he opened the door to his car, a woman's sharp voice rang down from the church, "We know who you are, buster! We know *exactly* what you want!"

Bailey slid into the seat. "Good," he said. "Now tell me."

The streets were murderously slick now, the traffic barely crawling—small accidents, cars off the road everywhere. Bailey drove aimlessly, distracted and given over to thinking about Jill again because he couldn't seem to think about anything else anymore, no matter how stupidly predictable and juvenile that was and no matter how acutely he was aware of those facts. So he missed his chance to get into the turn lane that would have taken him to his daughter Kate's house, where he more or less meant to deliver the pumpkin. Instead, he found himself drifting with the jammed traffic until it deposited him near the street where Jill lived, as though he had intended to go there in the first place—which he was reasonably certain he had not.

It was a neighborhood of older, boxy, split-entry homes. Many had been rentals since the oil boom years and looked it. But Jill's—the one she shared with her husband—was well kept, with a low hedge of arctic pea surrounding the yard and cedar planters on the porch steps filled with late chrysanthemums now wearing little crowns of snow. Jill was only a tech at the pump station, and her husband did something at home with computers that Bailey didn't think sounded profitable. He had an idea that the plain, sad house was all they could afford.

He pulled up across the street. He had never been to the house before exactly, though he had been on this street several times when, senseless with longing, he had driven past trying to catch a glimpse of her. One morning that summer, he had spied her through her front window, seated with her husband at their dining room table drinking coffee from blue mugs. And once he had passed when Jill was out front, kneeling on a green foam-rubber pad weeding the base of the hedge along the sidewalk, and she had looked up as Bailey rolled by, though he hadn't signaled or called out to her, and her mouth dropped and her trowel fell from her hand. But now she was at the pump station in the frozen mountains and would be for another four days. He stepped out of the car and straightened the breastplate of the devil suit.

Holding the pumpkin, looking at Jill's house, he found that he was glad, on some level, that she lived in such a meager place because it played into his dreams of the two of them together in something vaguely more interesting and stylish. He was not proud of the ungenerous thought, but more and more he was beginning to see that now, this far into it, some things were going to enter his mind whether he wanted them to or not. Fantasies? Oh yes, he'd had all the fantasies. The one in which Ann died suddenly, and Jill abandoned her husband to comfort Bailey. The one in which Jill's husband died and Bailey left Ann to be with Jill. The one in which Jill's husband *and* Bailey's wife died in unrelated accidents. And the one in which they perished together in a tragedy so absurdly coincidental that Bailey could hold it in his mind for only a few seconds, even on his very worst days.

He started toward Jill's house. Groups of trick-or-treaters cruised the sidewalks. A pair of teenage boys carrying pillowcases and wearing no real costumes but some black soot on their faces pushed past him and went up the steps and hit the doorbell. Jill's husband leaned out the door wearing a white dress shirt and jeans. He frowned at the boys. "Great costumes, guys," he said. "I can see you put a lot of effort into them." He dropped candy into their pillowcases, and they turned without a word and hurried back past Bailey toward the next house.

Bailey waited for the door to close, stepped up onto the porch, and bent to set the pumpkin between two pots of mums, wondering what Jill would think of it and the mystery of its appearance there on her porch. And when she told him about it the next time they spoke, he would let her go on and he would smile and finally admit that it had beeen his doing, and then let her decide which was more fantastic, the pumpkin or his placing it there.

In the middle of this thought, the door opened. Jill's husband had a cordless phone lodged between his shoulder and ear, a bowl of hard candies in one hand. He waved a fistful of the candies out the door, waiting for Bailey to give him something to drop them into. Bailey felt a current of panic climb his legs as he stood there clutching the pumpkin to his stomach. His face went hot inside the mask. Jill's husband looked up from the phone. He said, "Hold on a sec, Ma." He stared into Bailey's eyes. "You know, pal, some things are best left to young people." He reached out, lifted the lid off the pumpkin and dropped two candies in. As the door closed, Bailey heard him say into the phone, "I'm telling you, Ma, these holidays depress me. *Everyone* wants in on the action."

Bailey went back across the street to his car. He decided maybe he wouldn't tell Jill about this after all.

There was one last person he needed to talk to, though, and as he headed for the mall and the campaign headquarters, his mind was on what he would say to Ann if he were to tell her. *If he were to tell her.* This was not new territory for him, and every time he had the daydream in which he explained to Ann how he'd met Jill, and what he had said and what Jill had said, the same words—"one thing led to another"—came to him, and he paused, disturbed by the thought that the most interesting and exciting moment of his life was truly best described by a cliché.

At the mall, Bailey took the pumpkin out of the car one more time. He adjusted his mask and walked toward the doors, where two uniformed security men stood. One of them, a tall black man with round wire-rimmed glasses and a goatee that made Bailey think of jazz, swung the door wide for him but stood in the opening. He said, "No masks." He nodded toward a sign on the door with the same two words on it.

"What mask?" Bailey said.

"Very funny, sir." The guard let his hand rest on the Mace canister hanging from his belt.

"Listen," Bailey said. "I'm not going into any stores."

"Correct," the guard said. His partner, a much older man with a pale pink face, stood tapping at a hearing aid that filled his left ear. He cocked his head to one side as the first guard said with finality, "No masks in the mall."

Bailey felt the wind on the back of his legs through the nylon tights. A single snowflake fluttered into one of the eye openings in the devil mask and stuck to his eyelashes for a moment before melting. There was no way he was going to take it off now. "I have something important to tell my wife."

The guard nodded and pushed his tongue against his cheek. "And that would be something that can only be said in a mask." He looked over his shoulder at his partner and rolled his eyes. The older man shrugged.

"As a matter of fact, yes," Bailey said. "Really, she's right over there at the campaign headquarters." Hands full of the pumpkin, he pointed with his rubber-masked chin toward the red, white, and blue bunting at the far end of the mall.

The guard at the door turned to look in that direction, and Bailey made a quick move to step around him, but the older guard lunged. At the same time, the first guard threw his arm out to block Bailey and instead caught his partner across the throat with a chop right out of a kung fu movie. The older guard sank to his knees, gasping. The other one dropped and held him under the arms. "Breathe!" he said. "Come on, man, breathe."

Bailey was inside the door and saw his chance. He began walking briskly, putting distance between himself and the guards and heading toward the campaign headquarters. When the guard yelled, "Hey, hold it!" Bailey surprised himself by bolting, the pumpkin bouncing heavily against his stomach as he ran past the B Dalton bookstore, the T-shirt and the sneaker stores, past the attractive young woman at the ear-piercing kiosk. People were turning, looking up from the children before them in strollers, looking up from their cinnamon rolls and orange drinks, turning away from display windows and from the shiny red pickup truck with the price sticker in the window on its revolving platform. They turned to stare at the devil running through the mall.

Behind him, Bailey heard the guard shouting, "Halt! Halt!" and fleetingly wondered if the man had a gun. But he was on his way now, moving in the right direction at last. And so he ran, his pointy devil tail thumping against his back on each step, the soles of his shoes slapping against the red quarry tile floor and echoing down the mall.

On his way, he was. And as he rounded the corner across from the campaign headquarters, he was moving at a pretty fair clip for a fifty-six-year-old petroleum engineer carrying a very large pumpkin. He was sweating now, and the mask was slipping down his face, and his vision was limited to one eye. But he did see Ann talking on the phone at her desk just inside the headquarters window beneath the bunting. And out in front of the headquarters, he did see the little orange plastic warning cones and the man wearing coveralls lifting the mop from the yellow plastic bucket on wheels, and he did see the slick of soapy water spreading across the tile floor. And so he knew exactly what was happening when he felt his feet fly out from under him and his arms shoot out for balance. And he knew what he was hearing when the pumpkin sailed from his hands and exploded against the thick, tempered plate-glass window just above Ann's head with a blast that sent her lunging from her chair as though struck from behind.

But just because he saw what was happening, that didn't mean, in any way, that he could change or stop it then, and so there was truly nothing he could do at that point but marvel at his own reflection in the election headquarters window, looming suddenly huge before him, red and scaly and horned, arms and legs flailing in a crazy, grotesque dance. And in the last small fraction of the second before he hurtled into the pumpkin-smeared glass, his eyes met Ann's gaping back at him in recognition and terror, and—his mind finally clear of Jill at last—he heard himself thinking, Careful, Bailey. Careful now. This is one of those times a man could *really* make a fool of himself.

Maximum Reception

The morning after his retirement party, Delton went out and bought the satellite dish. He paid cash, made arrangements for its delivery, returned home, and sliced a six-foot-square patch out of his front lawn where he thought the thing should sit. All morning, he worked on the hole for the pad, rolling up the sod and hauling it to the curb, fighting the root webs and nested glacial rocks as he dug deeper. It was a warm June day, the solstice sun high over the Chugach Mountains east of Anchorage, and Delton was sweating fiercely when his wife, Fay, came down from the house and stood by the gaping excavation.

Delton had told her he wanted the dish, but he hadn't made it clear how much concrete would be needed to support it. He watched her survey their otherwise tidy yard: the lush iris beds, the peonies, the big weeping birch tree with its willowy branches sweeping right down to their fine lawn. She paused a moment and took in the little mountain ash tree she had planted the autumn before, smiling, Delton supposed, at the memory of it festooned with bars of perfumed soap to ward off the browsing neighborhood moose. She stared into the hole at the exposed dirt, the ends of worms, then directly at Delton.

"You think it's going to be that much better than cable, Del?"

"We've got to stay in touch, Fay," he said. He leaned against the handle of the shovel and mopped his brow with his hanky.

Fay looked at him closely.

"You'll get used to this, Del. It's going to be all right—really."

Delton knew she meant to be reassuring, but there was something in her voice that sounded a lot like pity too.

The satellite dish was the biggest residential model the store sold. Delton had asked about the really big units for hotels and apartment houses, but the salesman assured him the one he'd bought "would bring in everything that was out there."

"I guess you'll be needing an installer?" the man said. He produced a business card from the breast pocket of his sport coat.

Delton had worked on dams, pipelines, every kind of road and bridge in Alaska, but this was a little technical, *electronic*. He took the card:

J. RONNIE COOVER

Communications Adviser

Anchorage, Fairbanks, Juneau

There were three phone numbers. When he tried the local number, a message machine said the call had been forwarded to Fairbanks, that Coover would be checking in by remote. Delton was impressed. J. Ronnie Coover was clearly a man comfortable with technology. Delton left a message and spent the rest of the day working on the hole in his front lawn.

Just before supper, the delivery truck pulled up. Two young men with ponytails and muscles like melons wrestled the big steel halves of the satellite dish off the truck. They set them on the grass next to the driveway. Delton hustled to off-load the smaller boxes and coils of wire. Then he fetched three beers. He and the boys stood in the driveway and drank, swatting the mosquitoes rising from the lawn.

"It's a big one, isn't it?" Delton said over the rim of his beer can.

"Heavy fucker," one boy said. He set a sneakered foot on the edge of the dish.

The other boy looked at the pit Delton had dug. "Installing it yourself?"

Delton smiled. "Mostly."

It was the best he'd felt since the party.

As they cleared the dinner table, Fay said, "You're pushing yourself a bit, aren't you, Del?"

He knew where she was heading. She was going to want to talk about it, about him and what was on his mind. It was her way, and he didn't really mind it in small doses. He liked it, in fact. But if he was going to be home all day, every day, now, well. . . .

"I'd like to get the concrete poured in case this Coover guy can wire the dish right away. That's all," Delton said.

"Is that why you've been out there all day?"

"Fay, I'm doing fine."

"I heard more from you when you worked out in the bush."

Delton pushed back from the table. He didn't want this to turn into anything more than it had to.

"We'll talk about this later, OK? I have a couple of things I want to get done yet."

He went outside and worked into the evening, taking advantage of the lingering solstice sun, cutting the hole deeper and deeper, making room for the pea gravel and concrete that would support the dish. It was 11:30 when Fay called him from the porch: J. Ronnie Coover was on the phone from Fairbanks.

"Caught me between jobs," Coover said in a high, metallic voice. "I'll be down straight away to pick the spot for the dish. Don't pour the pad yet."

"But I got a place all cleared."

"It's got to be right. That satellite is in a stationary orbit up there. It's geosynchronous. Either you're aiming at it or you're not."

Delton shifted the receiver to his other ear. He looked out the window at the big hole in the middle of his front yard. He already had the bags of concrete mix stacked up next to it, the hose, the wheelbarrow to mix it in. He wondered again if he could figure out the electronics himself. A bulldozer, yes. A grader, a steamroller, no sweat. But he could barely operate the microwave. The VCR mystified him. Geosynchronous?

"You still with me? " Coover shrilled.

"I only got so much yard."

"I'll be right down," Coover said. "Next flight, for sure."

Delton hung up the phone.

"Another hole?" Fay said.

He sank into his big chair in front of the TV, clicked the set on, and grazed through the channels with the remote, then turned it off again. "This guy's the best there is, Fay. Coming all the way down from Fairbanks. If he says we have to dig a bit more . . . "

Fay stood at the screen door, glumly looking out at the wrecked yard.

"This is all new to me," Delton said. "I'm trying to get used to it."

"Me too," Fay said. "It's new to me too. Come on. Let's get some sleep. I don't imagine our Mr. Coover will be here before morning."

"You go on ahead," he said. "I'll be right up."

He wandered outside to look at the dish one more time. He stepped down into the big hole he had dug, pressed his hands flat against his lower back, and peered up at the pink evening sky until it made him dizzy wondering about that stationary orbit. How could anything hang there in one spot without moving and without falling back to earth? The idea made his head hurt.

Out in the bog behind his house, wood frogs struck up a disjointed squawking. He listened to their ragged song for a moment, then limped back inside. He set the alarm carefully for seven and crawled into bed next to Fay.

Delton woke to the sound of a car door slamming in front of the house. He sat up, disoriented. The daylight coming through the curtains seemed to be the same intensity as it had been when he'd gotten in bed. He was uncertain whether he had even fallen asleep, though the clock on the nightstand read 2:25. Someone outside was shouting in a high, tinny voice. Delton got to the window in time to see an orange taxi swerve away from the curb. There was a young man standing in his driveway, wearing a flannel shirt hanging out over his jeans. Fay was snoring softly. Delton grabbed his pants and ran downstairs.

J. Ronnie Coover was rooting through one of the half-dozen big, steel toolboxes, battered and plastered with airline stickers, that lay at his feet. He was young—in his early twenties, maybe—and had a wispy, first-growth beard. One earlobe was crammed with fine, gold loops and what appeared to be a fishing lure, but Delton had been on construction long enough to know that wild looks meant nothing when the work started; some of these young guys could work circles around the job vets.

Coover smiled up at Delton and continued poking through his tools until he came up with a compass and something that looked like a sextant. He stood and offered his free hand.

"Caught the last flight of the night," he said, once again startling Delton with the strained pitch of his voice. "I love dish jobs."

"You want to put your stuff inside until morning?"

Coover looked up at the sky. The sun was igniting the sky behind the mountains to the southeast.

"It *is* morning."

He took off across the front lawn at a brisk pace, walked right by the big pit Delton had dug, and stopped closer to the house. He looked up again, held the instrument to his eye, and jotted something in his notebook. He laid the end of a tape measure on the grass and extended it a yard or two until it was nearly touching Fay's mountain ash.

"Here we go," he said. "Give me a hand."

Using four wooden stakes and heavy white cord, they roped off the new location for the concrete slab. The mountain ash was just inside one corner of the square.

"We get that little tree out of the way, we got it knocked," Coover said, his voice cutting through the neighborhood like a siren. "Maximum reception!"

Fay had planted the mountain ash for the Bohemian waxwings its berries attracted. Birding was one of the things she suggested they take up when Delton retired. "Let's make a list," she'd said. "For our new life." She wrote Travel, Bird-watching, Gardening. Delton poked at his sheet of paper for a few minutes, his mind a desert, then copied Fay's.

Delton and Coover worked until 6 A.M., assembling the two halves of the dish on the lawn. Then, when it was clear that there was nothing more they could do until the ash tree was moved and a new hole dug for the concrete pad, Delton talked Coover into taking a break. Coover pulled a tiny Japanese TV out of one of his toolboxes and plugged it into the outlet on Delton's porch. They sat watching the news and talking quietly. Delton was pleased to hear that Coover had been on some big jobs—the Performing Arts Center, the museum downtown. Like Delton, Coover had worked out in the bush too, in the native villages, the mining and lumber towns. They traded stories about miserable superintendents, know-nothing architects. Around seven, they heard Fay in the kitchen fixing breakfast.

Delton tried to work up a smile as he broke the news about her tree.

"Move it? In midsummer? It's roots are working full-time," Fay said.

Delton mumbled something about reception.

Fay turned to Coover.

"What 's wrong with the roof?"

"Dish is way too big. First wind'll rip out the trusses. Saw it happen in Juneau."

"The back yard?"

"Mountains will block nearly everything."

Fay pinched the bridge of her nose. She leaned back against the counter.

Delton examined his napkin. Coover stirred in his chair. "Got to make a call," he said. He walked out of the room, punching numbers into the cellular he wore on his belt.

"Look, Del," Fay said quietly, "he seems like a nice enough boy and all, but he shows up here in the middle of the night and wants to cut my tree down."

"To *move* it," Delton said. "We need to move it a bit."

Fay brushed that aside. "You already dug a hole the size of a grave out there. I'm trying to be reasonable. Is this what it's going to be like from now on?"

Delton heard Coover go out the front door.

"I don't know, Fay," he said. "These things are complicated. They're complex."

"What's it going to be next week, Del, and the week after that? A tunnel? Pyramids?"

Delton got up from the table. "I'll talk to Coover," he said. He headed for the door.

"Coover?" Fay said. "It's not Coover that needs talking to."

Delton joined Coover on the lawn. They stood looking at the little ash tree, but his mind was on Fay. Maybe he *was* moving a little fast.

"This is coming between you two," Coover said, as though he'd read Delton's mind. "I'll step aside for a while, go see a friend here in town, get some sleep maybe. I'll call you later."

"You could sleep here," Delton said.

"Here's my cab now."

Coover started down the driveway, waving at the approaching taxi. He ran around to the passenger side.

"You talk it over with the missus. Let me know what you want to do." He paused, leaning across the roof of the cab. "Could auger a hole, drop a pole in it, some concrete, mount that big sucker up on top, maybe." He shrugged. "Might work."

Delton turned and looked at the dish. He tried to visualize it up on a pole, high above the tree and the yard. When he turned back, Coover was gone.

It was close to noon when Delton pulled back into the driveway. Strapped to the door handles of his old Cadillac was a six-inch-diameter black steel pipe that extended out beyond both the front and rear fenders. Small red flags flapped at each end.

Fay stood to one side and watched silently as Delton untied the front end of the big pipe and lowered it to the driveway. He cut the other end loose and let it fall with a fierce clamor, then hustled around to the trunk and hauled a heavy gas-powered auger out and set it next to the pipe.

"What in God's name?" Fay said.

Delton's hip ached, his back ached, his shoulders throbbed, but he couldn't stop smiling. He leaned close to Fay and whispered, "The beauty is, the tree won't have to move."

Fay looked at the long spiral blade of the auger. "Not even going to ask," she said. She turned and walked toward the house. "I'll fix some lunch."

When she came back out to tell him the food was ready, there was a cloud of oily blue exhaust hanging over the yard. In the middle of it, Delton stood drilling a hole in the lawn a few feet from the mountain ash. She watched the black soil curl off the auger bit as it corkscrewed deeper into the earth. Delton could see that she fully expected the little tree to disappear as its roots became entangled in the machine.

When he backed the auger out, he had a neat round hole.

"Perfect, isn't it?" he said. "The dish'll clear the tree by ten feet, and it'll be years before the branches even reach it. Then we can just sort of prune around it, you see?" Delton glanced at his watch. "I just wish Coover would call."

Suddenly a yawn came over him that he couldn't stifle, and Fay took him by the arm. "Come on, buster," she said. "You didn't sleep at all last night. Lunch, then it's nap time." She led him back up to the house.

He walked along in a daze. A nap? To the best of his knowledge, he hadn't taken a nap since he was five years old. Why didn't she just embalm him?

"I don't think I can sleep," he said. "I really don't."

———————

All afternoon, Delton paced from the yard to the house and back again, convinced that there was something he could be doing while he waited for Coover to call. He tried sitting by the phone, but lasted only a few minutes before going out to look at the newly augered hole once more.

Fay was asleep on the couch, her needlework on the floor nearby. In the window above her, the afternoon sky had turned a sour gray. Rain was beginning to streak the glass at a sharp, wind-driven angle. The house felt cold.

Delton covered Fay with an afghan and stood looking at her. She looked so stiff and so still, her mouth slightly open. She could sleep, he thought. He wondered if he'd ever want to again. He looked around at the room, trying to remember the last time he had a whole afternoon with absolutely nothing to do. He wandered back out to the front yard.

The neighborhood was quiet. A trace of rain glistened on the empty street. A gust of wind tore at the mountain ash, twisting its leaves to expose their silvery undersides. A corner of the tarp he had placed over the concrete sacks flapped furiously, and he walked down and put a rock on it.

The rain began in earnest then, and it felt good. It felt like a thousand cold, wet mornings on job sites from the Aleutians to the North Slope. He could smell diesel and the hot asphalt of a new road. He could smell sawdust and plywood and oiled concrete forms, and he felt his blood racing.

He pulled back the tarp and heaved a sack of concrete mix up into the wheelbarrow, ripped it open, ran the garden hose into it, and stirred it with the shovel. When it looked right, he poured the soupy mix down into the augered hole. Then he went for the pipe.

But the pipe was too long, too awkward, and way too heavy for one man, young or old. He had to drag it to the hole walking backward, grasping one end between his ankles. Pain shot from his neck to the soles of his feet. He felt the lack of sleep suddenly, as a fluttering in his eyelids.

Positioning one end of the pipe at the rim of the hole, he hurried to the other end and hefted it to his knees, jerked it to chest level, and pinned it there as it snagged on the lip of the hole and stalled. He heaved it up to his shoulder but could go no further.

The rain became a downpour, carried on gusts that bent the little ash tree almost to the ground. Dense drops lashed his face. He felt his feet sliding on the wet grass, the pipe slipping through his palms.

The dead weight of it—at first a matter for his back and legs—was now beginning to tell as a quivering in his chest and shoulders. He felt his pulse throbbing in the big artery in his neck where it pressed against the pipe. His ears began to ring. Spots circled at the backs of his eyes.

He found himself thinking about all the projects he'd been on over the years, how they hadn't seemed like anything but tasks to complete at the time, but how they now looked like pieces of a life. He cut a glance at the satellite dish lying on the lawn, the tools and supplies all around him. He wanted badly to finish this job, but the pipe was driving him into the ground.

Then the wood frogs started up, the racket growing as though the satellite dish had already begun funneling and focusing the sounds of Delton's new life.

There was something else too. A blooming, color-flooded vision forming. Delton squinted at the strain. He felt something give, and a welling up in his chest, and he closed his eyes to the flowering pain and saw Fay leaning out over the porch railing. She was wearing a yellow dress, tight and shapely over her hips. Her hair was dark and long, the way she'd worn it when she was young, free and blowing in the wind, her lips as red as the mountain ash berries.

She called out, "Delton," and it came to him, over the wind, the rain, and the frogs—maximum reception—and Delton pushed once more, the pipe as weightless now as time itself.

Q Roo

Rafael, with his nine years at Punta Morena Lodge, is the senior guide and as such gets first pick of the newly arriving clients each Saturday. So now he has no one to blame but himself that he will spend every day for the next week in a small boat under the fierce Caribbean sun with these two men who so desperately hate each other.

It is Sunday, the first morning of fishing. Rafael is sitting in the shade of the guides' palapa with his wife Lupita and their two-year-old daughter, waiting for his clients to come to the boat lagoon. He and his wife are not talking, having just had another argument—much the same as every other one they've had recently. It is Lupita's third season at Punta Morena, and she is not happy there. She doesn't like the isolation, doesn't like working with the simple little Mayan women at the lodge. She misses her sisters and her mother back in Tampico. She misses her friends, the night life, dancing, maybe an occasional movie. Things to do. Things to choose from. Here, she points out, there are only two choices: sand or jungle. Most of all, she doesn't like anything about the lodge's North American clients or the way they treat Rafael, and she has told him so again today. "If you want to be a servant, we can go clean houses in Texas," she said. They haven't spoken since.

Rafael is about to try to reason with her once more when the two clients come down from the lodge. They are father and son, and this alone might explain the tension he sees in them. But Rafael considers himself a bit of an expert on the behavior of the very rich, and talking to them now, he's convinced that something else is coming between these two, and he's beginning to think that this week he will truly earn his eleven American dollars a day.

Introductions are made. The clients talk about the weather, their bumpy flight down from Cancun the day before with their wives. As always—though he doesn't ask—they bring up their occupations. When the older man, the father, Charles, tells Rafael that he produces music videos in a city called Toronto, Rafael smiles and nods, though all he has heard of Canada is that the fish are large and the weather is terrible. Which is why he hopes that maybe these two can handle the big tarpon and permit and the incessant wind there on the flats, and is why he chose them. Because a client who catches fish is a client who tips well. And whether Lupita understands or not, this is, after all, his job.

As they talk, Rafael looks over their tackle and notices with dismay that everything they own is brand new. When questioned, Charles confirms that they have never fished salt water. Yet when Rafael asks what they'd like to try for first, Charles says, "Whatever. As long as I get a grand slam."

Rafael hopes for a second that it is a joke, but he can see that it is not. He sees Lupita frown and look away across the lagoon. With an effort he keeps his smile in place as he faces Charles.

"Señor," he says. "To catch a bonefish, a permit, and a tarpon all in one day is like a little miracle. In these waters it happens only eight, ten times a year, maybe. I don't know . . . "

"You've got six days," Charles says with casual effrontery, and wades out to the boat and sets his gear in it. Rafael hears Lupita suck her tongue against her teeth. He follows Charles to the boat and doesn't look back.

Charles is tall and thin, maybe fifty years old, but in good shape and youthful with his ponytail and diamond ear stud and crazy flowered shirts. Rafael had watched him earlier that morning at dawn, jogging past the guides' cabanas on the little two-track jungle road that connects the lodge with the Mayan Chac Mool ruins several miles down the coast. And though Rafael has seen such antics before, he was once again amazed that a man, even a North American, would voluntarily run nowhere in particular.

The younger man, the son with the unusual name of Troy, is as heavy and soft as his father is not. He is in his mid-twenties but seems almost a child—though all the guides are talking about his long-legged wife, the young redheaded woman who went snorkeling in the lagoon the day before in a swimsuit that would make a Brazilian blush. Troy has no opinions on where or what they should fish for, and now as they prepare to set out, he is more interested in the osprey hovering over the lodge pier than in the discussion of fly patterns. While Charles shows Rafael a box of crab imitations, Troy peers at the fish hawk through binoculars large enough to use for an anchor.

Rafael sees some possibility in that. The weather looks bad, and he almost certainly will not produce the grand slam that Charles seems to think he has paid for, but he can at least humor the young one's interest in the wildlife. But when he begins to answer Troy's questions about the big saltwater crocodile that sometimes appears beneath the lodge pier at night, Charles says, "Troy, if you wanted to go to the zoo, you should have said so." And when Charles then turns to Rafael and rolls his eyes as if to say, "Why have I been cursed with such a fool for a son?" Rafael reminds himself that he has six more days with these two, and he shakes his head as though he knows exactly what Charles means.

As he starts up the outboard, Rafael turns and sees Lupita watching. She is making that little mouth, the way she does when she is certain she is right about something. He waves, but she just takes their daughter by the hand and walks back toward the lodge. Not for the first time, he thinks he should never have brought her there.

Rafael runs open throttle into the wind for nearly an hour, the fiberglass hull hammering the waves, fly rods rattling and clacking in their Velcro holders like a Caribe rhythm section. The two men clamp their hats between their knees and clutch the edges of their molded plastic seats, arms and necks glossy with Bullfrog. The young one turns and gapes at every sight, attempting to raise the binoculars from time to time but managing only to hit himself in the forehead or nose. He's delighted by the black dolphins that momentarily cavort in the bow wake, a lone flamingo wading among new mangrove shoots. His father stares ahead.

When they round the island rookery of the frigate birds, Rafael cuts the outboard, and the skiff plows to a halt in the lee. He wipes the salt spray from his glasses, snugs on his Punta Morena Lodge cap, and reaches for the long fiberglass boat pole as he has done a thousand times before. Charles steps up onto the casting deck, rod in hand, stripping line in sloppy loops over his feet. There is no discussion between father and son over who will fish first. There is no discussion between them about anything, as far as Rafael can tell. Why do these families insist on traveling together? He has seen it a hundred times and still has no idea.

"Señor, strip the line down into the boat," he says, as he climbs up onto the poling platform above the motor. "That way you don't step on it."

Charles turns to him. "Do I look like an idiot?"

Rafael shrugs. Who knows what idiots look like in Canada?

The young one has spotted the frigate birds now, as Rafael pushes them past the island. The mangrove trees are heavy with them, the females clustered near the waterline, the big black males perched in the higher branches vying for their attention. "Look at those air bladders!" Troy says, pointing at the males' huge scarlet throat sacks ballooning out. "The size of them!"

"Hey, Audubon," his father says. "You mind if we let this $400-a-day guide find us a fish? Or shall we work on our life lists?"

Rafael isn't sure what a life list is, but he gets the message. They're paying $400 a day—each. And as much again for their wives, who will stay at the lodge all day doing whatever it is such women do with their endless free time. Charles acts as if he can't guess how little of that $400 Rafael sees, as though he has no idea how much it costs to operate the big Cessna Caravan that flew them to the lodge, the generator that keeps the overhead fans moving the dense sea air through their bedrooms at night, the bottled water flown in for the ice in their Cuba Libres. Never mind how much goes to both the federal and local Quintana Roo police and military agencies that keep the region safe enough that their half-naked gringa wives can loll around the beach roasting themselves like sand lizards. But who knows how their minds work? Anyone who would spend $3,000 a week to catch fish and turn them loose again is clearly not using the thought processes of a normal man.

Troy says, "Is that an ibis or a spoonbill?" He points to a smudge of pink in the dense green mangroves. "I think that's a spoonbill."

Rafael doesn't know the names of all the birds, doesn't get clients who look up into the trees much.

"Does *anyfuckingbody* care to fish?" Charles says. He gives Rafael a look. When he turns to face forward again, Rafael stuffs the pole into the sandy bottom and pushes a little harder than necessary. Charles almost comes over backward off the deck, doing a little dance on his fly line. He shoots Rafael another fierce glance, but he also takes the time now to set the line loops down into the hull behind the casting deck.

OK, Rafael thinks. *Está bien.*

He puts aside all troubling thoughts and sets off across the flats, letting the familiar push-and-glide rhythm of the poling take over now as he begins looking for the shadows of fish against the piebald sand and weed-blotched bottom. Up front on the casting deck, Charles stands taut, scanning the water. With his ponytail jutting out the back of his long-billed hat, he looks like one of the big wading birds.

It is work, Rafael tells himself, and not the worst in the world. He thinks of his brother back in Tampico grunting over an engine block, oil running down his arms like black sweat, his cousins wrestling their taxicabs through the choking Mexico City smog. True, Rafael's clients are a nightmare sometimes. But even so . . .

The frigate bird island shrinks behind them as he pushes on across the choppy flat toward a line of palms a mile ahead. Troy has been quiet since his father snapped at him. Now he points straight up and says, "Are those wood storks?" He has one hand extending his hat brim, the binoculars in the other fist. His jaw dangles. "They are. See the black wing tips?"

"Jesus," Charles groans.

Rafael looks up and sees three large white birds crawling across the wind-tortured clouds, legs stretched out behind them. He's seen them countless times, he supposes, never thought about a name for them.

"How do you say it?" he asks Troy. "Stokes?"

"Storks. Wood storks."

Rafael says it a couple of times. As he looks up at them again, he catches a motion out of the corner of his eye and turns to see a large permit passing behind the boat, dorsal fin just nicking the surface as it panics and disappears. He almost shouts out to Charles, but the fish is long gone, so he pushes on, furious at himself for missing that chance. Troy is now asking him something about sea turtles. "Green turtles or hawksbills?"

Charles looks back over his shoulder at his son as if he's stumbled upon the most discouraging sight he's ever seen.

Rafael tries to keep smiling, but it's not easy.

By midweek they haven't touched a permit, haven't even seen a tarpon, and some of Rafael's best spots look as though they've been vacuumed clean of everything but stingrays and small sharks. Whatever is going on between the two men has apparently deepened. The young one, Troy, speaks only to Rafael—about the birds, the dolphins, every small fish they see. Each day he asks about the crocodile, says he's looked for it every night under the dock but hasn't seen it. "Where does it live all day?" he asks. Rafael tries to humor him without setting Charles off.

When Charles speaks at all, it is also only to Rafael—usually to complain about the wind, which has not let up for one minute the entire time, or the clouds, whose scudding shadows make it harder than ever to see through the froth. He is not happy about the few small bonefish they have caught, and though all the other guides and clients are doing poorly too, Lupita overheard Charles asking the lodge manager about getting a different guide for the rest of the week.

"And you think these people are your friends?" she said.

"No, Lupita," Rafael said. "I think they are our life."

To make things worse, a new low-pressure system has smothered the bay, pushing the fish out beyond the reef. Rafael thinks about attempting the deeper ocean flats, but in this chop he would never be able to stay on the platform. So he presses farther into the mangrove channels, where the wind is more manageable and you never know what you might run across: robalo, mutton snapper, barracuda. Anything is possible, he tells himself.

They finally get a shot late Wednesday afternoon. After a horribly slow day, Charles has stepped down off the casting deck in disgust, and Troy has just climbed up when Rafael sees three permit tailing over a small coral mound. He maneuvers the boat so the wind is coming across Troy's right shoulder, and when everything is perfect, he whispers, "Cast, señor." Troy immediately wraps his backcast around Rafael's ankles and nearly yanks him off the poling platform. By the time the commotion subsides, the fish are halfway to Cuba. As Troy works to untangle Rafael, Charles shakes his head and sighs like a punctured tire.

Thursday goes almost as badly, though Troy does catch a nice barracuda that Rafael kills for dinner. When Rafael compliments Troy on the way he played the fish, Charles says, "Overblown pike." He climbs up on the deck. "Any time you're done screwing around," he says to Rafael, and glances down at Troy, who has rewarded himself with a beer from the cooler and is smiling for the first time in days.

"Christ, you'd think he was paying for this," Charles says, and turns forward again.

Troy's smile evaporates. He starts hiccuping and can't seem to stop.

Rafael thinks about reaching out with the fiberglass pole and tipping Charles into the bay, how wonderful that would feel. As always, he pushes on.

Lupita and the baby are waiting at the beach at the end of the day. As Rafael ties off the boat, Charles stalks off to the lodge, and Troy slouches away toward his room. Rafael holds up the barracuda and yells, "It is a good fish, señor." But Troy just waves from the hip without looking back, and Rafael finds himself standing there with the fish dangling from one hand, facing Lupita.

"Even when they catch something they're unhappy," she says.

"Don't start, Lupita."

Rafael kneels in the ankle-deep water of the lagoon and begins cleaning the fish a few yards from shore. A mob of lodge cats comes running from every direction, tails stiff with excitement. His daughter wades into the cats, petting them and pulling their ears as they mill along the water's edge yowling for scraps.

He feels Lupita watching him, but he doesn't look up from his work. "You know what I think?" she says.

He does not ask her what she thinks.

"I think you *like* being with these people. I think that when you're with them, you believe you are rich too."

That does it. He throws the half-filleted barracuda at her feet, and the cats swarm over it. Lupita sweeps the baby up and backs away from the melee as Rafael pushes past and heads down the beach.

By the time he is a mile from the lodge, Rafael has gotten over the tightness he feels in his chest every time he fights with Lupita. She is wrong, he tells himself. Yes, he has to humor them at times, weather their moods, and find them the fish they've paid so much to catch—even on those days when the fish truly do not want to be found. But how else can he earn the tips that make it possible to survive? And what are the alternatives? The maquiladoras that pay fifty cents an hour to assemble portable telephones so Americans can drive and talk at the same time? Or would she be happy in a hut on the beach, living with the buzzards and iguanas like the locals? That's what he should tell her: The beach has everything you need! You want a water jug? Go down to the beach—you may have to scrape a few barnacles off it, but plastic never rots. You want sandals? There are enough on this stretch alone to outfit an army. Netting? Rope? Miles of it. A hairbrush? Take your pick.

Rafael looks out at the rumbling Caribbean, curling wave on wave into the pink-white sand. Somewhere out there, all this unwanted stuff has been discarded. Maybe it comes from the cruise ships, those bloated floating monstrosities he has seen urgently steaming in and out of Cancun and Cozumel as if leisure were something you had to pursue. Not watching where he is stepping, he puts his foot into a puddle of soft tar, as common now as the plastic litter. Shit! These are not beach-found sandals he is wearing. These are the high-priced "reef walker" wading shoes a Japanese client gave him, along with his polarized sunglasses and a $200 tip. It was the best week of fishing, and the best money Rafael has ever made. Now the blue neoprene shoes are streaked with black tar.

He hurries inland for a hundred yards over the scrub-covered dunes and down to the jungle road. Cursing Lupita, the North Americans, and all the uncooperative fish in the sea, he rushes back toward the lodge for a quarter mile until he comes to a smaller two-track that veers off to the cenote, an ancient well in the spiny bedrock of the island. The water in the spring is no good any longer, and the old windmill and pump stand unused and rusted, but there might be gasoline or maybe even some

WD40 in the storage shed, and Rafael wants to get to it before the tar stains are set beyond hope.

The cenote road is almost grown over, jagged salt grasses tufting between the remnants of the tire tracks, jungle trees and vines enfolding it on both sides and shutting out the sound of the surf behind him. He can just hear the windmill blades creaking in the sea breeze in the clearing ahead and, as he approaches, something else. Voices. A woman laughing. A man says something but starts to cough fitfully. The woman laughs again.

He steps softly now until he can see the windmill through the foliage. Below it, sitting on the low stone wall that surrounds the cenote, is his client, Charles, and with him is his son Troy's wife, the young redhead. They are smoking a joint, passing it back and forth, choking and laughing. The woman leans into her father-in-law suddenly, and they rock back so far that Rafael thinks they will surely fall into the well and become dinner for the hideous blue crabs that swarm the mossy stone walls beneath the surface. Charles's hand comes around the young woman and cups one breast, and she hoots with laughter. She is wearing a bright-patterned skirt that is barely a sash across her hips, and even from that distance, Rafael can see the white V of her underpants as she kicks those long tanned legs.

He backs away down the path, heart surging. His wading shoes will have to suffer. This is a sure way to lose his job. The woman's muffled laughter filters through the trees, and he is suddenly reminded of being with his own Lupita at a certain cottonwood grove along the river outside Tampico. When was the last time they shared such hilarity? He would apologize and be extra nice to her this evening.

Later, his ruined wading shoes are drying on the steps of his cabana as he lies in bed listening to the throbbing pulse of the surf and trying not to think about what he has seen, trying not to think about the unfortunate young man Troy. He pulls Lupita closer against him and drifts into a dream in which he is wading on a sandy flat covered with schools of permit and tarpon. Then, by some dream logic, he is up to his waist in the tepid cenote, the crabs watching him with their horrible black eyes, and he cries out and cannot fully awaken. He thinks he feels Lupita patting his leg softly, rubbing the back of her hand against his thigh, and he finally floats back into the dream of the flats. But the fish are gone.

Friday morning Rafael waits alone at the boat lagoon for Charles and Troy. Lupita has chosen to stay at the cabana. "I can't stand to watch you kissing their buttocks any longer," she said as he left the house.

He promised her that he would consider quitting the lodge, think about moving back to Tampico to work in his uncle's tire shop. But now as he fuels the boat tanks, he mutters to himself, thinking that what he should have said to her was, "You want to try living without money?" He likes the sound of that and says it again and stares out at the Caribbean beyond the reef. It is calmer now than it has been in days, and above it the vast blue sky looks like it never held a cloud in its life. He checks his watch. The other guide boats have already left for the flats, but there is no sign of his clients, and he is beginning to wonder if there will be any fishing today at all when Troy shows up alone and climbs into the boat.

"Your father coming?" Rafael asks.

Troy says he doesn't know. He looks out at the sea too, and his mouth hangs open like it often does, but it is devoid of wonderment now. He doesn't even turn to look when the resident osprey smashes into a school of snappers near the end of the pier.

"Did you go down to the dock with the flashlight last night?" Rafael asks.

Troy seems not to hear.

"The crocodile was there again. Hillario from the kitchen told me."

Troy still doesn't turn around. He reaches down and picks a bit of seaweed off the floor mat, drops it over the side.

"They feed him chicken heads," Rafael tries. "Crocodiles love chickens. I don't know why."

"There's no crocodile," Troy says.

"Oh, I see," Rafael says. He knows this is a good opportunity to avoid involving himself with this client and his many problems, yet he hears himself saying, "You know, amigo, we don't *have* to go out today."

Troy turns in his seat. Hope appears on his face for a second, and then it's gone again when his father comes stalking through the palm trees and down to the boat.

As Charles gets in the boat, Rafael studies him for any sign that his involvement with the young woman is affecting him. But Charles looks relaxed, rested. He looks like a man who has caught a fish of a lifetime and then slept very well. He rubs his palms together and says to Rafael, "Another day in paradise, as they say, eh?"

Rafael pulls on the starter cord and reminds himself that next week—if he is still working there—he will have all new clients to choose from.

The sea is as calm as it gets at this time of year, and he runs them all the way to the three large islands called Tres Marias. If the fish return to the shallows today, they will be here. He stops the boat close to the nearest island and climbs up onto the platform.

For the first time that week, everything feels right. The tide slack, the wind dead, the water a quivering blue window into nothing but possibility. There is a real chance that everything could change today.

Charles stands and takes a step toward the casting deck first, as he has every morning, but Troy already has his rod in his hand and cuts his father off. Troy is heavy and not at all graceful, and he trips and nearly goes over. He catches himself with his free hand and finally gets upright. Charles stands there a moment looking at his son's back. He turns to Rafael and raises his eyebrows, but Rafael just leans on the pole and focuses on nothing. Charles looks off to one side, gives his ponytail a little tug, and returns to his seat. The only sound is the fitful clicking of Troy's reel as he strips line into the boat.

Rafael hasn't poled them a hundred yards when a large black form noses out from around the point of the near island. He jams the pole into the bottom and pins them in place as a broad-beamed military launch pulls across their path. The man at the wheel blows a whistle he has hanging around his neck, and from a tunnel in the mangroves, four more men wade out in the waist-deep water and haul themselves over the gunwales of the big boat. In spite of the heat, they're wearing black fatigues and black hats and heavy ammunition belts for the automatic rifles they carry at ready. They never take their eyes off Rafael.

He waves at them casually, but he can feel his knees starting to swim. When the big boat turns toward them, he climbs down from the platform and straps off the pole to hold them there.

"What is it?" Charles says. He gawks at the launch the way Troy does at turtles and egrets. "Police?"

"*Marinas*," Rafael says.

"No shit?" Charles says. He leans back in his seat, hands locked behind his head, elbows wide, beaming like this is a colorful local ceremony they've trotted out for him. "What are they doing?" he asks. "Looking for somebody?"

Rafael says, "They are always looking for somebody, señor."

The launch pulls alongside, engine chugging ominously. Everything is black, the boat, their uniforms, their guns—everything except the silver whistle the captain wears around his neck, where it glints and flashes in the sun as the marines silently study them. To Rafael's horror, they throw him a line.

When they are tied off, the captain speaks to Rafael in Spanish for a minute. He has information that someone is using a lodge boat to run cocaine into the interior by way of the labyrinthian mangrove channels rimming the bay. Rafael listens attentively, all the while considering that the men with their guns pointed at his knees earn less than half what he is making as a fishing guide. He says, as humbly as he can, that he can't imagine anyone crazy enough to try such a thing.

Charles is clearly oblivious to the fact that Rafael is faint with fear and the knowledge that—this far from shore—these men answer to no one. Still smiling that offensive smile of his, Charles says, "What did he say?" as though the captain of the marines is a jabbering primitive.

Rafael tells Charles, in English, what the captain said.

"Smuggling? In a lodge boat?" He laughs. "That's positively ludicrous."

The captain stiffens. He turns and looks at Charles, lifting the whistle to his lips and pursing them against it lightly. With a nod of his head, he motions Troy down from the casting platform and into his seat. Then the captain leans so close to Troy that he seems about to whisper something in the young man's ear, but he just lifts the binoculars off the seat and hangs them over his own neck alongside his whistle.

Charles can't resist laughing. "Perfect," he snorts. "This guy is perfect."

Rafael suddenly feels cold—an odd sensation in the middle of the shadeless Caribbean. "Señor," he says to Charles. "This is not a laughing matter."

Now the captain wants to know what the North American said.

Rafael considers the possibilities. He knows this boat. A year ago it drifted, powerless, into the lagoon in front of the lodge, manned by two seasick and sunburned Panamanians. They offered no explanation for their presence there, paid Rafael a wad of cash to fix the engine, and chartered the lodge plane to Cancun. They said they'd be back for the boat. Rafael was just finishing the repairs when the federal helicopter arrived on the beach with a squad of men dressed and armed much like this group here before him. He ended up piloting the boat all the way to the naval station at Cozumel with their guns at his back. They questioned him for a day, frightened him half to death, and gave him just enough money for the ferry to Playa del Carmen. Now it is their boat.

Again the captain asks him what Charles is smiling about. The captain is very young, barely older than his men, and he seems nervous and edgy. Rafael can see that if anything goes wrong here, *everything* is going to go wrong.

He looks at Troy, ashen and trembling in his seat. He looks at Charles. Charles is still amused by it all. *Because he can afford to be.* Rafael understands now. That's the difference between father and son and the trouble between them. No amount of money will make Troy that rich. And it is certainly not a problem Rafael will ever have to face himself—no matter where, or how hard, or how long he works.

He says to the captain, "The North American thinks your ideas are a joke, and that you are absurd."

———————

Charles finally stops smiling when they put him in the big launch. He rants and threatens and keeps screaming something about the Canadian consulate until he's drowned out by the roar of the twin engines as the marines leave the smaller boat rocking in their wake.

Rafael and Troy watch the launch grow smaller and smaller until it melts into the saw-toothed horizon, far beyond the reef where the waves never subside. For a minute, neither one speaks.

An orange-capped gull falls from the sky and hits the water a few yards off the bow and comes up with a small needlefish scissored in its beak. As it picks up off the surface, a frigate bird swoops out of nowhere, knocks the fish free, and snatches it in midair.

Another moment passes as they watch the birds go their separate ways, the gull whining mournfully, the frigate bird chuckling. The surface of the water looks like it has never been disturbed.

At last Troy says, "We have to get back to the lodge and report this."

To Rafael's ear, Troy doesn't sound particularly urgent.

"Sí," Rafael says. "We do. But it is early yet and such a fine morning."

He ships the pole, starts the outboard, and sets off toward a small mangrove island where he knows of a pelican nest low enough to see into from the poling platform. He will show Troy the comical baby pelicans and then, nearby, a bay where horseshoe crabs come to die by the hundreds. He will show him an unexcavated Mayan altar, where a stone-carved "descending god" seems to plummet headfirst through the thick jungle greenery like a falling coconut. He will show Troy where the crocodile sleeps.

All these wonders are in the opposite direction of the lodge, yet, as he has said, it is a beautiful day and still early. And really, he thinks as they set out across the great bay, what is there ever back on shore for a man but work and trouble, trouble and work?